Fabric Art
Journals

QUARRY

First published in the United States of America by
Quarry Books, a member of
Quayside Publishing Group
33 Commercial Street
Gloucester, Massachusetts 01930-5089
Telephone: (978) 282-9590
Fax: (978) 283-2742
www.rockpub.com

Library of Congress Cataloging-in-Publication Data

Sussman, Pam.
   Fabric art journals : making, sewing, and embellishing journals
   from cloth and fibers / Pam Sussman.
       p.   cm.
   ISBN 1-59253-196-2 (pbk.)
   1. Altered books. 2. Textile fabrics. I. Title.
   TT896.3.S9 2005
   702'.8'1—dc22   2005007991
                                                    CIP

ISBN 1-59253-196-2

10 9 8 7 6 5 4 3 2 1

Design: Laura H. Couallier, Laura Herrmann Design

Photography: Allan Penn Photography

Illustrations: Pam Sussman

The illustrations that appear on pages 40–41 originally appeared in
1-2-3 Embroidery: Easy Projects for Elegant Living (Rockport, 2003),
and were drawn by Judy Love.

Printed in Singapore

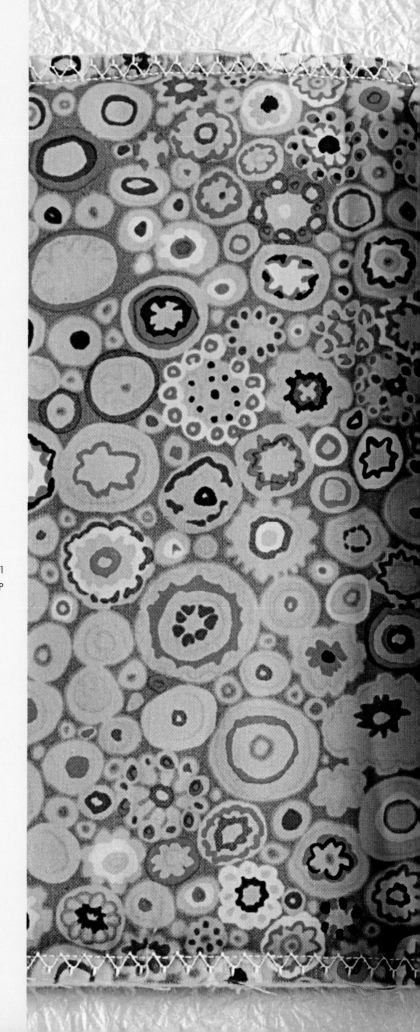

GLOUCESTER MASSACHUSETTS

Fabric Art
Journals

Making, Sewing, and Embellishing
Journals from Cloth and Fibers

Pam Sussman

QUARRY BOOKS

CONTENTS

INTRODUCTION

My path to becoming
a **FABRIC** *journal artist was first*
paved with **PAPER.**

I had been making, and teaching others how to make, artists' books from paper supplies for nearly ten years when, one winter day, I was seduced by a child's cloth book. A television craft show I watched had featured an accomplished quilter who took novelty fabrics and turned them into a wonderful library for a new grandson. The little books were charming, but what excited me most was the concept of instant illustrations. Talented fabric designers had already done the hard work of creating beautiful drawings and patterns. All I needed to do was decide how to put them together!

This revelation led to a whole new road of artistic pursuit. I quickly learned that the skills I had finely tuned from years of traditional bookbinding did not work on fabric journals. The predictable characteristics of paper, such as "if you fold it, it will crease" no longer held true.

My first fabric book was a sorry attempt to marry a paper book structure with cloth. The covers were rigid, the pages were overstuffed with the wrong support material, and it sprang open far more eagerly than it stayed closed. It was, however, the beginning of my journey to explore a whole new universe, and my second book was much improved.

As I took my growing stack of fabric journals along to paper book classes I taught, I observed how quickly people became engaged with these soft little books. They turned and explored the pages with their fingers, savoring the tiny details of stitching, buttons, and beads, marveling at the explosion of color in the combinations of cloth. Fabric books simply beg to be touched and experienced through the hands as well as the eyes. My seduction turned to full-blown infatuation, and I have been in love with this art form ever since.

The more fabric journals I made, the more I discovered that I did not need to abandon the skills I acquired making paper books. I found so little instruction available for making fabric journals that I set out to create a collection of projects that would help other artists jump into this emerging craft. Whether you are a paper book artist looking to explore new materials or a fabric artist or quilter who has never made a book, I hope you will use this collection as your ticket to explore a whole new dimension of tactile visual expression.

Pam Sussman

Chapter One

FABRIC JOURNAL BASICS

Your journey begins with a
simple TOOL KIT *and an understanding*
of FABRIC BASICS.

Whether you approach making fabric art journals from a quilting/fiber arts or a paper arts background, the good news is that you may already have some of the tools needed to begin. For those who love to acquire useful tools (and I count myself in this group!), you'll find taking on a new craft project is the perfect opportunity—or excuse—to add to your collection.

Fabric journal tools are, by and large, the tools of the art quilter, and so are the basics of measuring, cutting, and sewing. Much of the information in this chapter will be familiar to quilters and fiber artists, so feel free to move through this section quickly. The challenge for art quilters making a first book will be learning how to work on a very small scale, as well as how to work in three dimensions.

For the paper-arts book maker, a few tools, such as the cutting mat and ruler, will be familiar, but you may need to add a few sewing tool basics to your kit. Some tools, such as the rotary cutter, will require a little practice before you can achieve good results. If you've always paid attention to details such as careful measuring, you'll do very well when you transfer these practices to fabric. Be sure to read the information that discusses working with fabric versus paper, as it will be of special interest to you. Over time, you may find that you enjoy working with the fabric artist's tools enough to adopt their use in your paper arts projects as well.

ARTIST: Teesha Moore

Fabric Journal Tools

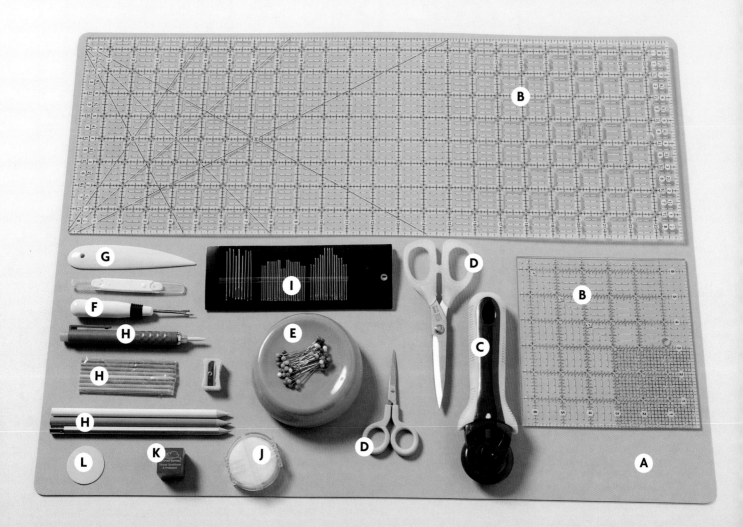

The tools of the quilter are used
to make most fabric journals.
A sewing machine is optional.

A visit to the quilting section of the fabric or craft store will yield all the tools needed to create fabric journals.

Cutting Surfaces (A)

Cutting mats come in many sizes; a good choice for making fabric journals is 18" × 24" (45.7 × 61 cm). On most mats, both sides of the board can be used for cutting. Measuring grids on cutting mats are helpful in general but not highly accurate. Protect the board from heat and direct sunlight, and always store it in a flat position so that it does not warp.

Measuring Tools (B)

Quilter's rulers are ideal for use with rotary cutters and come in a variety of lengths, widths, and markings. Fabric journal artists will find a large ruler (24" × 8½" or 6" [61 × 21.6 or 15.2 cm]) useful for cutting cloth for pages, and a quilter's square (6½" [16.5 cm]) handy for cutting small ends and pieces. Clear ruler markings and ¼" (0.6 cm) increments are important features; nonslip backing is an extra bonus that will improve cutting accuracy. Paper book artists may find they prefer these rulers to traditional measuring tools for paper projects as well.

Rotary Cutter (C)

This rolling, circular blade on a handle can cut through multiple layers of cloth and batting at one time. The 45-mm blade is standard; larger and smaller options are available. Choose a rotary cutter with a comfortable handle and a protective shield with a locking mechanism for the blade when not in use. These cutters are extremely sharp and should always be used with care.

Scissors (D)

Sharp, medium-size scissors for cutting cloth and a small pair of detail scissors for clipping threads are all that you need to make fabric journals. Pinking shears are a fun, optional tool for finishing page edges and for appliqué.

Pins (E)

Quilter's pins are suitable for making fabric journals, and a few dozen will be an adequate supply.

Seam Ripper (F)

Choose a cutter with a sharp blade and a well-defined point for lifting individual stitches.

Point Turner (G)

Paper book artists can substitute the bone folder for this tool, used to gently push out the corners of sewn seams into a nice, neat square.

Marking Pencils (H)

There are many types of marking tools: pencils, markers, and chalks. Avoid water-soluble markers; they are intended for fabrics that will eventually be laundered. A chalk holder with multiple color refills and a sharpener will serve most fabric journal needs or, in its place, a selection of quilter's pencils in several colors.

Needles (I)

Look for an assortment of hand sewing needles that includes sharps, betweens, embroidery, and tapestry needles. Specialty needles (such as beading needles) may be useful for specific projects.

Beeswax (J) and Thread Conditioners (K)

Used on thread, these sewing aids help reduce tangles and allow thread to glide easily through fabrics.

Needle Gripper (L)

This textured, rubber piece will help pull needles through multiple thicknesses of fabric.

Fabric Journals versus Paper Journals

Comparing Techniques and Materials

Paper book artists who have never made a fabric art journal are in for a few surprises along the way.

In a paper book world, everything cuts neatly with a craft knife. With precise measurements clearly marked onto paper materials and with careful cutting, an exact result can be produced time after time. When a sharp crease is needed, paper is scored, folded, and burnished with a bone folder. Papers and boards are joined together with wet glue or by sewing, and the final project goes into a book press, producing a neat, finished product.

The fabric journal maker learns to live by different rules. Raw materials, with differing fiber contents, handle differently, sometimes unpredictably, and nothing is quite so precise. Fabric has a life of its own, and the successful fabric journal artist learns to appreciate and work with these nuances to create a book unlike anything that can ever be produced with paper.

Differences in Measuring and Cutting

Hard surfaces such as paper and board are measured and cut with clean, sharp edges that stay sharp. Because fabric is woven of many individual threads, a clean, sharp edge is only a reality for a few moments after cutting. Although excellent cutting and measuring tools exist for fabrics, cut fabric edges will fray no matter how accurately they are prepared. The less cut edges of fabric are handled, the less they will fray. One strategy is to sew a cut edge as soon as possible after cutting.

Differences in Folding

Fabrics can be folded and creased, like paper, but the tools for the job are different and so are the results. The steam iron is the replacement tool for a bone folder. A single thickness of fabric will hold a crease fairly well. When additional layers are added, such as interfacing or batting and a backing layer of fabric, crisp folds become more rounded. A multilayer fabric fold can be defined with a row of stitching that will help the fabric layers bend more easily.

Differences in Joining Surfaces

Sewing replaces the glue bottle in most construction aspects of making a fabric book. Paper artists not keen on using a sewing machine or fond of hand sewing can use one of the many fabric glues or fusible adhesives to join cloth layers together. Fusible adhesives can be used to attach linings, interfacings, trims, appliqués, and edge bindings, and they work using the heat of an iron to activate the glue. It is entirely possible to construct a fabric art journal without sewing a single stitch.

One Final Difference

Paper book artists making their first fabric journal may heed this final piece of advice from someone else who has been there: Relax, and enjoy the process. Fabric journals take much more time to complete than most paper-based books. While construction of the book itself is no more time consuming than making a comparable paper book, the page and cover embellishment process can be very labor intensive. You will probably spend far more time on this work than you ever thought possible. However, keep in mind that fabric journals are very portable, and can be worked on while watching television, listening to a lecture, or traveling in the car.

Hand Sewing versus Machine Sewing

The decision to sew fabric journals by hand or by machine is purely personal. From a practical viewpoint, all the sewing needed to make a journal from cloth can be done by hand. Sewing machines offer the obvious advantage of doing the task much faster, with stitching that is stronger and more uniform in appearance. Still, there is something quite enchanting about a book that has been created completely by hand.

Hand sewing has the benefit of being very portable. It's possible to take a page or two along in a little bag and work on the project between appointments, during travel, or while spending time with family. Machine fans will celebrate that the speed of the sewing machine makes it possible to complete a project in a timely manner.

It may be that you will end up using a combination of machine and hand sewing to create your journals. Basic seaming and construction—the unseen work—can be done efficiently by machine, leaving more time for the appliqué, embroidery, and other embellishing to be completed by hand.

Even the most basic sewing machines have sufficient features to make the task easier: straight stitch, reverse stitch, and a zigzag stitch. Added features such as a buttonhole stitch, an appliqué stitch, and a few decorative stitches will add value to the machine as an art tool. High-end embroidery machines can take your journal making to an entirely new level of lavish embellishment, if that is your desire.

Whichever approach you choose, make your journals using the best craftsmanship you can bring to the party. You will savor the process and appreciate the end result for a long time.

Accurate Measuring and Cutting

The quilter's measuring and cutting tools are ideal for cutting fabric journal pages, and their proper use practically guarantees success each time. Three tools are needed: a cutting mat, a quilter's ruler, and a rotary cutter.

Measuring

The grid on the cutting mat is useful for lining up material edges, but it is not accurate enough to use as a measuring tool. Most grid mats are printed on a rubberized surface, which can fluctuate with its surroundings. Some grids are printed with thick lines that, while easy to see, make it impossible to get a precise reading.

The markings on the hard surface of the quilter's ruler, however, remain true and should serve as the measuring authority. When choosing a quilter's ruler, look for incremental markings and numbers that are clearly defined and easy to read. Beyond clear markings, a nonslip surface on the back of the ruler will improve cutting success. Some rulers have a nonslip surface built in, or you can cut and apply a clear, nonslip material (such as Invisigrip by Omnigrid) to the back of any quilter's ruler.

Cutting

Control is an important element in accurate cutting, so choose a rotary cutter that feels good in your hand. Cutters can have dual, right-, or left-hand orientation; the cutter blade always rolls with the exposed side of the blade against the edge of the ruler. Follow the manufacturer's directions for the correct assembly of the blade in the handle.

Change the rotary blade frequently. Paper artists wouldn't think of using the same craft knife blade for months on end. Rotary blades are especially prone to nicks, created by rolling over pins, the edge of the ruler, and unseen objects on the cutting mat. Nicked blades will leave behind areas of uncut threads along the cutting line; worn blades will require more pressure to make the cut. For the best results, use the same brand of blade as the rotary handle. Design differences among the various brands make it hard to interchange or retrofit mismatched parts.

CAUTION!

· · · · ·

Always close the rotary cutter every time you put it down. The blades are extremely sharp.

When the tools are in good order, you are ready to cut. Always cut away from the body, either from bottom to top, or across the top of the quilter's ruler. Apply even pressure downward on the ruler with your non-cutting hand, and keep your fingers well away from the ruler's edge. Start the cut off the edge of the fabric, roll on and along the ruler's edge for the length of the cloth, then roll off the top edge. You should not have to bear down hard on the cutter to make a cut. Cut slowly at first until you develop a level of comfort in working with the tools. Practicing on scrap fabric will help improve your accuracy and speed.

Pressing

The Importance of Pressing

Pressing is to fabric journals as using the bone folder is to paper books: It provides the special finish that distinguishes good craftsmanship.

Not every fabric is meant to be pressed, and not all fabrics are pressed the same way. Never press high pile fabrics such as velvet on the front side of the fabric, and avoid pressing many synthetics with a hot iron. If you are working with 100% cottons, however, press with lots of steam and high heat. This helps impart a professional finish to the fabric surface. Never press over buttons, beads, metallic trims, or the heads of pins—all of these can melt.

A steam iron, spray water bottle, and pressing surface or ironing board are the tools needed for pressing. A craft-size iron may be a better choice than a full-size model, because its smaller size will allow for easier maneuvering around embellishments.

How to Press

Fill the iron with water and preheat it to the desired temperature setting. Place the fabric piece on the pressing surface, smoothing any folds or creases. Put the iron face down on the fabric and hold it there for a few seconds. Do not slide the iron around as you would when ironing a garment, because this may stretch the fabric edges. Lift the iron and put it down again in a different spot of the area to be pressed. Continue until pressing is complete.

PRESSING IS A THREE-STEP PROCESS:

1 Press the seam exactly as it was sewn.

2 Open up the seam and press it flat.

3 Press the seam to one side or the other.

How to Determine the Pressing Direction

- When working with light and dark fabrics, press the seam toward the dark fabric so it will be less visible.

- When several seams come together in a central point, press one side to one direction and the other side to the opposite direction to keep the seams open. This will reduce bulk at the intersection.

- When joining rows or strips of fabric together, press the seams in the same direction for consistency.

- Always press fabric before cutting it. If the fabric feels limp, spray it with sizing first, then cut it. Sizing is a fabric finish that adds body to the surface of the cloth without the stiffness of starch. It comes in spray cans and can be found at the supermarket in the laundry products section.

Finger Pressing

Sometimes it will not be practical to stop and press the seam with an iron. Use your finger, or use the flat side of the point turning tool much as a paper artist would use a bone folder to flatten the surface.

Choosing Fabrics and Thread

Unlike a wearable garment, fabric art journals will never intentionally see the inside of a washing machine. This allows for endless options in fabrics: They do not need to be colorfast or washable, and they can be as dissimilar in weight, texture, and opacity as desired. A carte blanche approach can incorporate nonfabric materials as well, including paper, vinyl, polymer clay, and virtually anything else.

Cottons are good for beginners because they handle predictably in sewing and pressing. Thanks to a recent surge of interest in quilting, there are thousands of options in pattern and color. Muslin is especially good for learning basic construction techniques. A muslin model of a new book structure will help identify areas that require special attention before cutting into your precious final fabric.

Once you have mastered the basics, move on to the more exotic fabric choices, such as silks, velvets, organza, antique linens, and more. As you venture beyond quality cottons, keep in mind that exotic fabrics require extra care in handling and sewing. These are some considerations:

- **Pressing** may not be possible for some fabrics. Follow the manufacturer's directions, usually printed on the bolt end of the material. Test a scrap first to determine whether the fabric can be pressed. Fabrics with a deep pile, such as velvet, cannot be directly pressed, but they can be lightly pressed on the back using a needle board. Vinyl will melt and permanently fuse to the iron.

- **Sewing machines** may need adjustment to accommodate special fabrics. Check the machine's instruction manual for the best settings to use on a particular fabric. Special sewing foot attachments, adjustment to the thread tension, foot pressure, and stitching width and length are some of the many options that can be changed to handle special fabrics.

- **Special needles or thread** are required for some fabrics. A general reference sewing book will help identify the characteristics and challenges of working with many types of fancy fabric, and it is a good addition to your bookshelf.

Threads

Many beautiful threads for hand and machine sewing are available. Here are some choices of interest for makers of fabric books.

- **100% cotton thread** is for hand and machine quilting. This thread is strong and dependable, comes in a wide selection of colors, and meets most basic construction needs.

- **100% polyester thread** is for hand and machine sewing. This general-purpose sewing thread is also available in many colors, although it is not quite as strong as 100% cotton.

- **Rayon thread** is widely used for machine embroidery. These threads offer brilliant colors with a fine gloss, and they produce beautiful decorative stitching. However, rayon thread is not as strong as cotton and is not a first choice for book construction.

- **100% silk thread** is for silk fabrics and is fabulous for appliqué because the stitching just seems to disappear. Silk thread comes in beautiful colors and is more expensive than cotton or rayon thread.

- **Heavy-duty thread,** such as button craft, is a mixture of cotton and polyester, and it is a good choice for attaching large buttons on bindings. Fewer color choices are available for this very strong, thick thread.

Inner Support

Nearly all fabric journals need some means of support between the layers of cloth. In addition to adding some heft to the pages, support material also helps to keep a single layer of fabric from tearing when attaching embellishments such as appliqué, buttons, and beads. The support material you choose will determine how thick the pages will be, how the pages will feel when they are handled, and whether the journal can be displayed in a standing position.

Interfacing

Garment makers have long used interfacing to support collars, cuffs, facings, and other critical stress points of clothing. Interfacing can be woven or nonwoven, and it comes in different weights ranging from light to heavy. Some are fusible on one or both sides; others are nonfusible. Each weight will impart a different feel to the page.

If you plan to attach heavier embellishments to the page, choose a medium- or heavier-weight interfacing. Otherwise, the choice of weight is mostly one of preference. Lighter weights of interfacing can be layered together to create heavier support.

Stiff Interfacing

Another choice for fabric journals is the very stiff interfacing developed for use in baseball cap bills. This is especially useful for cloth journals that will be displayed standing up, requiring extra support. The nonwoven, synthetic material is about $1/8$" (3 mm) thick and comes in both fusible and nonfusible versions. A popular choice with crafters for making fabric bowls, boxes, and handbags, this interfacing comes in 22" (56 cm) -wide rolls and is sold at many quilt stores.

Batting

When soft, "pouffy" pages are desired, batting is the solution. Used by quilters between the top and bottom layers of a quilt, batting adds both support and dimension to fabric journal pages.

Batting comes in varying thicknesses, described as loft, ranging from low to high with low loft at the thin end of the scale. The size of the project often determines which loft is selected: high loft for larger pieces with widely spaced sewing (such as a quilt) and low loft for smaller pieces with close stitching, such as art quilts or journal pages. Most batting is labeled with specifications for the desired spacing of stitches for a particular loft. Because most fabric journal pages are relatively small (compared to the size of a typical quilt), low-loft batting is a good choice for most cloth book projects.

Batting also comes in different fiber contents—100% cotton, synthetic (polyester), and wool—and in white or natural. It is sold by the yard or prepackaged in sizes for quilting or crafts. Do not confuse batting with stuffing, the loose material used to fill pillows or sewn dolls and toys.

Make a Sample Book of Support Choices

Visit the fabric store and purchase a small amount of different weights and types of interfacing and batting. Make up sample pages with each type, using the same fabric to cover the support material on all the pages. Label the page with the details of the support material (name, weight, and the like) so you will remember what was used inside. This sampler will serve as a handy reference when deciding which support material to use for a future project.

Basic Sewing Stitches

Hand Stitches

There are a few basic hand stitches you will use for almost every project.

Running Stitch

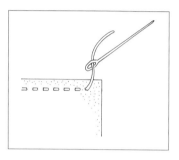

The running stitch is used to join two or more fabrics together. When it is used in place of the straight stitch on the sewing machine, the stitches should be evenly spaced and about 1/8" (3 mm) long. For joining, it is sewn with a double thickness of thread. The running stitch can also be used for top stitching and appliqué as a decorative element.

Basting Stitch

This variation of the running stitch joins fabrics together temporarily and is usually removed after the final sewing is completed. The length of the stitches can vary. Basting is typically done with a single thickness of thread in a high contrast color to the background fabric.

Back Stitch

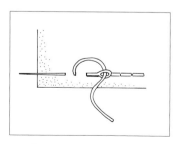

When a strong stitch is needed to join fabrics, the back stitch is very useful. The back stitch more closely resembles machine stitching in appearance, and it is a better choice than the running stitch for fabrics that are thicker. Back stitches should be evenly spaced and about

1/8" (3 mm) long. The back stitch is especially good for corners, because it stands up to the pushing and poking associated with turning fabrics inside out. A few back stitches taken at the beginning and end of a running stitch line will provide extra strength at the most vulnerable points.

Slip Stitch

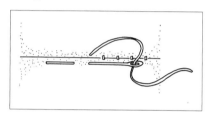

Two folded edges can be joined together almost invisibly with the slip stitch. This stitch is useful in joining the gap left in the seam when turning on a page with an enclosed seam. Because most of the thread is hidden in the folds of the fabric, only a small stitch is seen along the sewing line. Spacing for the slip stitch is about 1/4" (6 mm) apart for most fabric journal pages.

Machine Stitches

The basic stitches on a sewing machine are the ones used most for making fabric journals.

Straight Stitch

The straight stitch is used to join fabrics and is the machine equivalent of the hand-sewn running stitch. Most machines allow adjustment to the length of the straight stitch; the more stitches per inch, the stronger the sewing will be. The machine straight stitch can also be used for embellishment.

Reverse Stitch

Used primarily for reinforcement, the reverse stitch is used at the beginning and end of a line of straight stitching, and around corners.

Basic Edge Finishes

Simple sewing and embroidery stitches are all that you need to finish page edges in a fabric journal. A seam allowance of ½" (1.3 cm) will be adequate for these basic edges on most fabrics.

Enclosed Edge

Place the right sides of the fabric pages together and pin in place. Mark the seam allowance with a chalk pencil. Straight stitch along the seam guideline, leaving about 4" (10 cm) open along the bottom edge. Turn the fabric right sides out through the opening, using a corner finishing tool to square up the corners. Fold under the opening seam allowance and press, then close the seam with the slip stitch sewn by hand.

Pinked Edge

Straight stitch along the seam line, then use pinking shears to cut off the excess fabric approximately ¼" (6 mm) beyond the stitching line.

Zigzag-Stitched Edge

Straight stitch along the seam line, then trim the fabric beyond the stitching line to ¼" (6 cm). Use a sewing machine with a zigzag stitch to sew through all the layers of fabric on the seam allowance.

Blanket-Stitched Edge

Straight stitch along the seam line, then use embroidery floss and the blanket stitch to bind the raw edges together.

Whip-Stitched Edge

Straight stitch along the seam line. Fold the raw edge of the seam allowance in half, then use embroidery floss and the whip-stitch to bind the raw edges together.

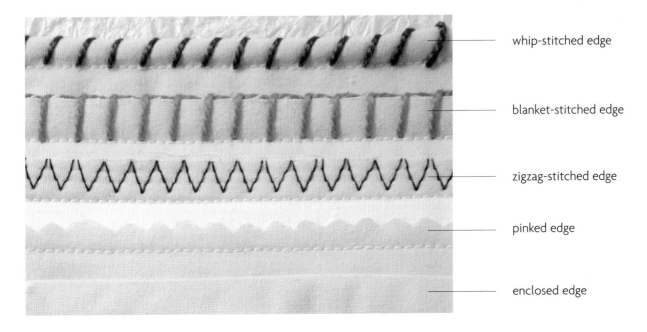

whip-stitched edge

blanket-stitched edge

zigzag-stitched edge

pinked edge

enclosed edge

Chapter Two

EMBELLISHMENTS FOR FABRIC JOURNALS

Constructing a **FABRIC** *journal gives you permission to enjoy the* **ICING** *before the cake.*

In many cases, you will want to completely embellish the pages of a fabric journal before they are joined together to form a book. Many embellishment techniques require access from the back side of the fabric page for sewing and other connections—tasks that are much easier to accomplish while the pages are still unbound as a volume.

A wide variety of fabric embellishment options are discussed in this chapter, with special attention to how you might use these techniques in an art journal. Many topics in this section—appliqué, embroidery, fabric painting, image transfers, and beading—have been around so long that it is possible to find many different books on each single subject. Use this section as a guidebook to areas you'd like to visit and, if you like what you see, by all means, continue your exploration with more advanced reading on the topic.

If you are new to fabric embellishment in general, making a cloth journal provides the perfect excuse to explore new techniques and processes. Some embellishments, such as embroidery, may trigger forgotten memories of attempting a craft long ago. This is your opportunity to revisit that earlier experience and now take it to a new level. Some of my best teaching moments have come when students discover they really enjoy working with materials they've never worked with before, or haven't used since grade school.

Fabric embellishment is wonderfully satisfying as a task. From a simple piece of cloth, a handful of beads, and some decorative thread come spectacular results. You'll spend many hours with the cloth, the beads, the thread, and the tools to achieve those results, but the end product will be well worth the effort. Enjoy "icing" your fabric pages in preparation for the final step—completing your journal.

ARTIST: Keely Barham

Tea-Dyeing Fabrics

Vintage-themed fabric journals are perfect candidates for aged cloth. Tea-dyeing adds instant age to basic muslin or cotton fabric. It uses no special chemicals or equipment, and can be done on the kitchen countertop. Within an hour, you can create an array of pastel-colored fabrics, ready to be cut for fabric art journals.

The kind of tea selected will determine the end color result, as will the strength of the brew. The more tea bags used, and the longer they are allowed to steep, the more intense the color will be. Different types of teas—even different brands of the same type—produce colors that range from antique gold to pale yellow to intense pink. Fruit teas create some of the more vibrant colorings; green tea blends produce more subtle results.

Tea-dyed fabrics dry much lighter than the color they appear to be when wet. Thus, you may

Instructions for Tea-Dyeing Fabrics

1 Wash and dry the fabric. Cut the fabric into 1-yard (0.9 m)- or half-yard (0.45 m)-long pieces.

2 Place about twelve tea bags in the large container and cover them with 6 to 8 cups (1.4–1.8 ml) of boiling water. Allow the tea to brew for 8 to 10 minutes, until it is very strong.

3 Remove the tea bags and add a piece of cloth to the solution. Turn or dip the fabric frequently to make sure it is completely saturated. Let it soak for 10 to 15 minutes, then check the color.

4 When the desired color is achieved, squeeze out the excess tea, rinse briefly under tap water, then place the fabric in the dryer with an old towel. It will take about 15 minutes for the cloth to dry. Some of the tea coloring may transfer to the towel during the drying process

5 Remove the cloth from the dryer, press it, and cut it to the correct size for the project. If the fabric feels limp and is hard to cut, spray it with sizing or starch, then iron it and cut it to size.

SUPPLIES

- SEVERAL YARDS OF GOOD-QUALITY, 100% MUSLIN OR COTTON
- ASSORTED TEAS
- LARGE CONTAINER, SUCH AS A MIXING BOWL OR PLASTIC DISHPAN
- POT OF BOILING WATER

orange and black pekoe blend

blueberry tea

peach tea

green tea

plain muslin

Give new life to old family photographs by incorporating them into a heritage-style fabric journal. Layer tea-dyed fabrics and embellish with antique buttons and lace, photo image transfers, and muted-color ribbons for a vintage journal page.

want to soak the fabric for a longer time, beyond when the desired color is achieved, so that the final result will be closer to your true color choice.

Treating the muslin or cotton with an alum soak prior to tea-dyeing can intensify and alter the results on some fabrics. Alum is often used to pretreat fabrics for marbling, because it helps the ink transfer more readily to the cloth. Use 1 cup (235 ml) of alum and 4 teaspoons (20 ml) of Calgon water softener to 1 gallon (3.8 L) of water. Soak the fabric thoroughly, squeeze out the solution but do not rinse, then air dry the fabric. When it is dry, proceed to the tea-dyeing steps.

Note: Do not use kitchen containers for the alum soak that are used for food preparation.

For less uniform coloring, fold the fabrics before adding them to the tea solution, or twist the cloth in spots and secure with rubber bands. Tea will become trapped in the folds and prevented from reaching all the fabric evenly, resulting in unusual color variations.

Variation: Coffee-Dyeing

When more intense color is desired, try coffee-dyeing. Place the cloth in a large bowl and pour several cups of strong, brewed coffee over it. Swish the fabric around in the solution to saturate the entire piece, then allow it to soak for 15 to 20 minutes. Rinse under tap water and dry, as instructed in step 4 of the tea-dyeing instructions.

Painting Fabrics

The canvas covers of these
sketchbook journals are
painted, stenciled, and rubber
stamped with acrylic paint.

Painted fabric has a special depth and beauty that manufactured cloth can seldom duplicate. Paint can add glorious color, interesting pattern, and surface dimension whether used to cover the entire background or to embellish selective details on a journal page. Use paint to add text, create the subject matter, or define areas of the page design.

Fabric painting as an art form has many applications, and many excellent books on this subject are available for further reading and exploration. Here we will focus on some basic painting techniques as they relate to the particular needs of fabric journal artists.

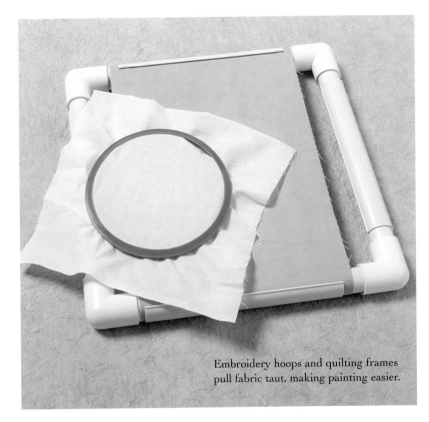

Embroidery hoops and quilting frames pull fabric taut, making painting easier.

Selecting Fabric for Painting

Because fabric art journals don't need to be colorfast or washable, feel free to paint on any fabric you choose. Inexpensive muslin makes a great painting surface; so does beautiful, more costly silk. Keep in mind that paint will add extra weight to the page, and may alter the surface texture from soft to stiff, depending on the type of paint used and the density with which you apply it.

PAINTING ON FABRIC IS A THREE-STEP PROCESS:

1 Stabilize the fabric by securing it to a frame or adhering it to a solid surface.

2 Apply the paint.

3 Cut the fabric to the project size.

Stabilizing Fabric for Painting

Fabric is easier to paint when it is taut; both paint and applicator are better controlled when the surface tension is firm. When stabilizing fabrics, always start with a larger piece of fabric than you need for the project. Any fabric can be temporarily stretched or stabilized for painting using these techniques.

Stretching Fabric on a Frame

A small, portable quilting frame is a convenient, temporary stretcher for fabric. The square-shaped, lightweight plastic tubular frame has snap-in-place sleeves that clamp the fabric to the frame, then remove easily when needed. The smallest size, about 11" (27.9 cm) square, is good for painting background fabrics and large areas of fabric journal pages. In place of a quilting frame, a sturdy embroidery hoop can be used. Hoops have the added advantage of coming in many different sizes, making them more suitable for smaller fabric pieces.

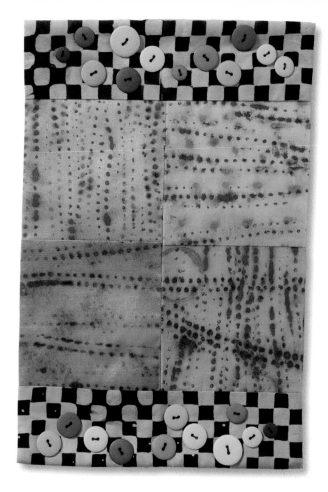

The irregular tracks on this painted sampler were created by dipping a textured dog toy in the paint, then rolling the toy onto the fabric.

Attaching Fabric to Paper

The same freezer paper that quilters use for paper-pieced appliqué is also useful for painting, especially for fabrics too small to fit on the quilting frame. Cut a piece of freezer paper the same size or just slightly smaller than the fabric piece to be painted, and place the shiny side of the paper down against the back of the fabric. Apply a heated dry iron to the dull side of the freezer paper, holding in place for a few seconds. The heat of the iron will melt the coating on the freezer paper, temporarily fusing the paper to the fabric. When painting is complete, peel the freezer paper away and discard it. Freezer paper is sold at the supermarket along with other food wrapping papers.

Selecting Paints

Virtually any acrylic paint can be used for a fabric art journal, since colorfastness is not an issue. However, the type of acrylic paint used will affect the way the fabric looks, feels, and behaves afterward.

- **Regular acrylic paints,** intended for canvas or paper, tend to make fabrics stiff. The effect can be softened by mixing the paint with acrylic medium before use. Medium comes in different finishes (matte, glossy, and satin) and different weights (heavy, medium, and light) as well as forms (fluid and gel). For most fabrics, lighter weight, fluid medium will impart softer qualities to the painted surface.

- **Acrylic fabric paints** generally produce a less rigid surface on painted fabrics. There are many different types of fabric paint: luminescent, metallic, opaque, translucent, and dimensional. It is a good idea to try a variety of paints on scrap fabrics to find the type that suits your style of painting and the desired end result.

Applying Paint to the Fabric Surface

Paint can be directly or indirectly applied to fabric using a brush, sponge, or found object with a raised or textured surface.

- **Brushes** made especially for fabric painting generally have stiff bristles to help push the paint into the woven fibers. Stencil brushes are usually round in shape, short in length, and very stiff, with flat-top bristles. A soft, wide bristle brush can be used to blend areas of color on a large fabric surface. A toothbrush and a wooden craft stick work well together as a splatter paint tool.

- **Sponges** for painting come in many varieties and vary in price dramatically. A hydrocephalic sponge is made of synthetic material that does not dry out, and it will retain its shape over time. Natural sea sponges and silk sponges from the decorative paint supply department of the home improvement store may prove too large for painting small fabric pages, so cut or tear them into smaller,

A selection of brushes and
sponges for fabric painting.

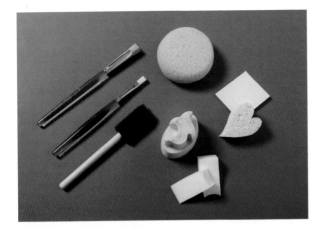

Found-object tools and
stencils can add dimension.

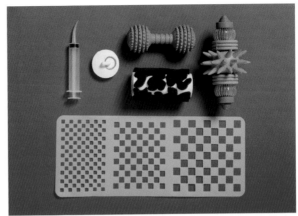

more manageable pieces for book projects. Pop-up
sponges from the kitchen or craft supply store can
be cut into shapes, expanded in water, and used
with paint to print surface patterns. Cosmetic
sponges from the health and beauty aids section
of the drugstore or supermarket are inexpensive
and the perfect size for working with stencils.

Found-Object Painting Tools

Found-object painting tools add interest and variety
to painting. Most paste paper artists have a special
stash of textured tools and objects used to create
patterns in the paste/paint mixture. The same texture tools can add fun and surprisingly sophisticated
results to fabric painting as well.

- **Textured paint rollers** from the home
  improvement store are an easy way to add clouds,
  leaf patterns, crackle lines, and other dimensional
  looks to a fabric background. Many of these
  rollers now come in small sizes, perfect for small
  fabric journal pages.

- **Hardware store finds** such as rubber drain
  stoppers and stair treads can add unusual texture.

- **Plastic disposable dental syringes** can be
  filled with paint and used to write or create
  designs with very thin lines.

- **Fabulous textured pet toys** from the pet
  store can be brushed with paint on the raised

surfaces and rolled across the fabric to create
random patterns.

- **Rubber stamps** with large solid surface areas
  work well using paint applied with a small
  disposable sponge brush. Fine-line stamps are
  less suitable, because the paint builds up in the
  small spaces between the lines, giving a less crisp
  impression. Use highly detailed rubber stamp
  images with rubber stamping fabric inks instead.

- **Stencils, manufactured and found,** used
  by paper artists, work just as well for fabric
  embellishment. Craft and scrapbook supply stores
  and the paint departments of home improvement
  stores offer a wide variety of stencils, and also
  sell blank stencil sheet material for making your
  own designs. Look again at flat found objects
  with openings as a source of unusual stencil
  designs. Netting, fencing, chicken wire, hardware
  cloth, drain covers, sink mats, and metal and
  plastic grids are just a few items to consider for
  found stencil materials.

Cutting Painted Fabric to Project Size

Always let the paint dry thoroughly before cutting
the fabric to the correct project size. If the stretcher
has left creases on the fabric, press them away on
the back of the cloth, not on the painted surface.

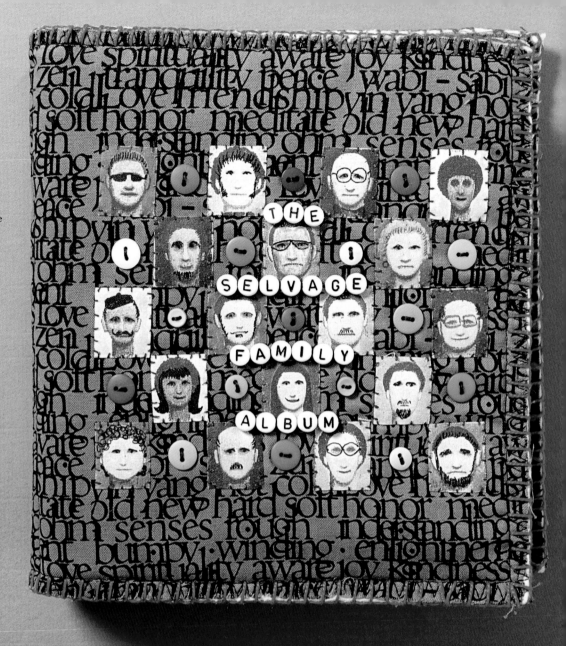

The title for this fabric journal was composed by sewing tiny letter beads to the cover. The background cloth uses typography primarily as a design element to create a pattern, yet the reader can still have fun picking out individual words from the body of text.

Adding Words to Cloth Pages

Fabric journal artists have a distinct advantage over the creators of quilts and wearable art—their projects never have to be laundered! This benefit allows a wide range of possibilities for adding text to the pages of fabric journals. Without the wear and tear of the water, laundry detergent, and washing machine to contend with, it is possible to use inks that are less stable and processes to embellish the pages. Paper book artists who are making fabric journals for the first time will find that many of their text-generating tools will work just as well for fabric journals.

Rubber Stamps

Use rubber stamps of famous quotes, titles, and other text to stamp onto a piece of fabric, then appliqué the stamped cloth piece to the background.

In addition to printed fabric, beads, markers, stencils, rubber stamps, and labeling tape can be used to create text.

Create personal text with a rubber stamp alphabet, stamping the words letter by letter. The uneven alignment of this lettering process adds a lot of charm to the finished page. There are many stamp pad inks designed especially for fabric use, but because colorfastness is not required for fabric journals, other stamp inks will work equally well. After the ink is dry, heat set the type by pressing with a dry iron.

Computer-Generated Text

The ink-jet printer and the computer are highly useful tools for making journals of fabric or paper. Computer-generated text offers the widest range of font choices, and the ultimate degree of control over word size, spacing, and composition. Compose the text on the computer, then print it out onto a variety of media choices: cloth sheets of canvas, cotton, or silk, or iron-on transfer sheets that are then applied to the fabric surface with heat. See the section on Image Transfers, page 31, for more details about this process and the materials.

Hand Lettering

It is possible to hand letter directly onto fabrics using inks or diluted paints with dip pens and flat lettering brushes. Calligraphy markers also work for direct hand lettering, although the colors tend to be less vibrant than those of inks and paints. Very fine-line fabric markers can be used to hand print or write directly onto the page. Apply hand lettering to tightly woven fabrics with a smooth surface, such as muslin, poplin, and canvas. It's a good idea to test the lettering medium and tools on scraps of the intended fabric to avoid surprises on the final pages.

Beads, Game Pieces, and Hardware

String together alphabet beads to form words, and then sew them onto the pages. Visit the scrapbook supply store for a large selection of metal letters, game piece letter tiles, and other small items with alphabets that can be sewn or otherwise attached to the page. Keep in mind that the weight of some metal embellishments, such as typewriter letters, may be inappropriate for the thickness of the fabrics chosen for the journal. Add extra support material such as a strip of interfacing to the back of pages that will carry items of substantial weight.

Stencils

Letter and number stencils come in many sizes and can be used with markers or paint. Like rubber stamps, these guides can be used to create individual text letter by letter, or used as decorative text elements in combination with letters created by other means. Stencil letters have a certain rough quality that adds boldness and contrast to the page. They can be especially beautiful when sponged with multiple colors of paint or ink, or used in a layered effect with other design elements.

The fiber scrap bag can yield some interesting source material for fabric journals. Tiny words were clipped from the selvages (edges) of cloth scraps and then appliquéd to the text pages as titles for this fictitious family album.

Embroidery

Use basic embroidery stitching, by hand or by machine, to add words to the page. The stem stitch is useful for hand embroidering letters; the satin stitch is a popular choice for machine stitching. (See the Embroidery section, page 39, for instructions on hand stitches for lettering.) High-end embroidery machines offer a large selection of typefaces and can be programmed to create any words on cloth, but this is an expensive option. Whether embroidering by hand or machine, plan the composition on scrap fabric before working on the final fabric.

Label Machines

The same labeling maker that helps organize files can also be used as a typesetter. Many manufacturers offer iron-on tape as a cartridge choice for their machines. Compose the text on the label maker keyboard, then print it out in long strips and cut them apart to fit the page design. Apply to the fabric following the manufacturer's instructions.

Woven Labels and Twill Tape

When only a few words are needed for the page or for a title, use commercially available labels with embroidered words and phrases. Twill tape, a tightly woven cotton utility flat tape, comes in a variety of widths and colors, some with preprinted text. Unprinted twill tape can be rubber stamped with words using a small alphabet, then sewn or attached to the page. These items are also found at scrapbook supply stores. Most fabric stores carry a selection of unprinted twill tapes in the notions department.

Printed Fabrics

Fabrics printed with text designs are becoming more common, and they provide an instant solution to adding words—or the appearance of words—to the page. Some fabric word possibilities can be found in the scrap bag. Don't overlook the words printed on the selvage of screened cotton fabrics as a fun way to create text. These printed edges usually list the name of the fabric design, the designer, and the fabric manufacturer. Collected over time, the words can be put together to form titles and phrases.

Special Markers

Laundry and Sharpie markers in fine-line and broad widths are about the fastest, easiest way to add words in personal handwriting to a journal page. Some markers are prone to spreading or bleeding on fabrics, so test the results on a scrap of fabric before applying directly to the final composition.

Mending fabric transfers provide less defined, vintage-looking results. Color can be added to this black and white transfer process with color pencils or chalks.

Image Transfers

Photographs and other two-dimensional art, traditionally the paper artist's media, can easily find their way into fabric art journals using image transfer processes. Pictures can be faithfully reproduced directly onto cloth that is cut, sewn, embroidered, beaded, painted, or otherwise embellished.

New interest in preserving and using old photographs has led to a blizzard of exciting materials and many reference books for making image transfers. Earlier methods often used toxic chemicals or labor-intensive transfer media. Today's

technology has made the process of transferring images to cloth as easy as making a photocopy. Don't be so quick to discard the old ways, however; part of their charm is the incomplete or slightly blurred image that often results from using low-tech reproduction methods. This may be just the effect you are looking for to enhance your journal pages.

There are many good, extremely detailed books on the subject of image transfers. Here we will touch on some of the many options that work well on fabric, from high to low tech.

A combination of photo fabric and iron-on transfer sheets create the base for this art quilt.

Transfer Basics

Nearly all of the transfer techniques use photocopies or printouts based on one of two technologies: toner or ink jet. Toner-based photocopies are those made on traditional black and white copiers or on laser copiers, both color and black and white. Toner is a dry powder that fuses to the paper with very high heat, and the powder can be transferred to yet another surface given the opportunity and the right materials. Toner-based equipment is typically found in most offices and at copy shops. The price of home office color laser copiers and printers has dropped dramatically in recent years, bringing it within the reach of more artists and making it possible to generate copy masters without a trip to the copy shop.

Ink-jet technology dominates the home printer and copier market at present; as a result, there are many more products available for image transfer using this format. Ink jet is a wet, water-soluble ink that is unstable for use with other wet media. However, unlike dry toner, ink jet can be applied directly to fabric, making it very useful for image transfer purposes.

Image-transfer materials for laser and ink jet are vastly different and cannot be used interchangeably. Use only the materials designed for your equipment.

A truly valuable piece of equipment for the fabric journal artist using many image transfers is a compact, all-in-one printer/copier/scanner with a digital camera card reader. This amazing machine allows you to transfer images from virtually any source: photographs, online images, copies, scanned artwork, digital clip art, and computer-set type. At under $100, these machines are easily affordable and greatly simplify the ability to make image transfers quickly.

High-Tech Transfers

At the top of the list for ease of use are photo fabric sheets. These sheets allow direct-to-fabric image transfers from ink-jet printers and copiers. They consist of fabric that has been pretreated to accept images, backed with paper to help carry the fabric through the printing process. Pretreated photo fabrics are widely available in craft, fabric, and quilting stores, with many optional features. They can be colorfast or fusible, in a variety of fabrics such as muslin, canvas, or silk, and in white or cream colors. These prepared sheets come ready to travel through your printer or copier and require no special settings. After the ink is dry, the paper backing is peeled away and discarded, and the image is ready to be cut, sewn, or fused to a fabric page.

Pretreating and Backing Your Own Fabric Sheets

The price of pretreated photo fabric sheets may be considered too costly by some to use in large quantities; if so, the cost per sheet falls dramatically by making your own pretreated fabric. Purchase high quality, 100% cotton fabric by the yard and soak it in an ink fixative, such as Bubble Jet Set 2000, following the manufacturer's directions. When the fabric is dry, iron it and then cut it into smaller pieces. Attach each piece to a backing sheet, such as freezer paper or full sheet label stock, and then trim it to size to fit the printer or copier paper tray. The sheets are used in the same way as packaged photo fabric.

Some ink-jet printers now use permanent inks that eliminate the need for using ink fixative. Fabric sheets are still cut, backed, and trimmed to fit the paper tray and used in the same way. Without the added expense of the ink fixative, this technology further reduces the cost per sheet of photo fabric.

Iron-On or Heat-Set Transfer Paper

This is a two-step transfer process for both ink-jet and laser-based formats—just be sure to purchase the correct supplies for your equipment! Transfer the image via copier or printer to the special transfer paper, then cut out the image and transfer it onto the receiving fabric using the heat of an iron. This type of transfer adds stiffness to the fabric and works best on white or light color cloth, unless the transfer sheet is specifically designed for dark background fabrics.

Medium Transfers

In this case, "medium" refers not to the level of difficulty required but to the substance used to make the transfer. Acrylic gel and matte mediums used by painters to extend and enhance the capabilities of their acrylic paints can also be used to apply images to many surfaces, including cloth. The process for using gel and matte mediums is similar. First, print the image on ink-jet transparency film. Brush the gel or matte medium onto the receiving fabric, then place the inked side of the transparency film face down on the fabric. Burnish the image in place until the transfer is complete. Images transferred with matte medium receive another protective coat of matte medium.

Other types of transfer medium, sold specifically for image transfers to many different surfaces, work differently. Brush the medium directly onto the image printed or photocopied on paper, applying several coats with drying time in between brushings. Next, soak the image in water for 20 minutes until the paper begins to soften and can be rolled off with your fingers. The resulting clear piece with the image intact can then be adhered to fabric or any other surface using another coat of the medium as a glue. Images are not limited to photocopies with image transfer medium; any matte surface image, including those from newspapers and magazines, can be used. Because of variations in the formulations of transfer mediums, it is best to follow the instructions provided by the manufacturer of the product.

TRANSFER TIP

• • • • •

Images that transfer from the top surface of a photocopy will appear in reverse on the receiving fabric. Thus, images with text will be unreadable. Make the photocopies or printouts in mirror image mode, an option on most copiers, to avoid a backward reading transfer. Direct-to-fabric transfers do not need to use mirror image photocopies.

Low-Tech Transfers

The old ways still work, and sometimes they provide exactly the effect you want.

Solvent Transfers

Some of the earliest image transfers were accomplished with toner-based black and white photocopies and a solvent such as acetone (nail polish remover), paint stripper, or mineral spirits. Place a fresh photocopy face down on the receiving surface. Apply the solvent to the back of the photocopy paper with a cloth, or by pouring it directly on the paper. Rub until the transfer is complete. Make solvent transfers in a well-ventilated area, preferably outdoors, using protective eye gear and gloves. Less toxic solvents such as Citra-Solve, Goo Gone, and Turpenoid will transfer a photocopied image. Colorless marker blenders containing Xylene also work for this purpose, and are more convenient to use and store than conventional solvents.

For good results with a solvent transfer, wrap the receiving fabric tightly around a hard surface and tape it securely in place. Tape the photocopy to the fabric before using the solvent. Movement of either fabric or photocopy will result in blurred or incomplete image transfers; this may be the desired effect in some cases.

Mending Fabric Transfers

My very first image transfers were made using this process, with toner-based photocopies and mending fabric sheets from the notions department of the fabric store. First, iron the mending fabric onto the photocopied image, using an iron setting for wool or cotton. Next, peel the mending fabric away from the copy. The mending fabric becomes a miniature printing plate, with the image transferred to its shiny surface. Apply the same mending fabric to the receiving cloth and use the iron to transfer the image again. Because mending fabric comes in relatively small sheets, image size is somewhat limited. Many artists made image transfers in the 1990s using this process, but most have now switched to the more convenient and less limiting photo fabric methods.

Appliqué

A century ago, appliqué needlework was highly prized for its neat, tiny stitches that were barely visible to the eye, in a perfect melding of the applied fabric piece to the background. Today, fiber artists appliqué with abandon, using exposed, frayed edges, uneven and exaggerated stitching, and nontraditional materials in a wabi-sabi approach to layering fabrics. This is not your grandmother's appliqué.

Appliqué can be done by hand or machine; each process has unique benefits. Machine appliqué is decidedly much faster and produces consistent results; hand appliqué, while slower to complete, is a wonderfully portable project that can go anywhere and allows for infinite variations in the stitching patterns.

A fabric journal inspired by the paintings of Mexican artist Frida Kahlo relies almost exclusively on the use of appliqué and colorful fabrics to tell its story. Cloth image transfers of the artist's paintings are sewn to intermediate-size panels of contrasting color fabrics that are in turn stitched to the background page fabric. The intermediate panels provide a visual buffer zone so that the detail of the paintings can be better appreciated against the vibrant, high contrast fabric backgrounds.

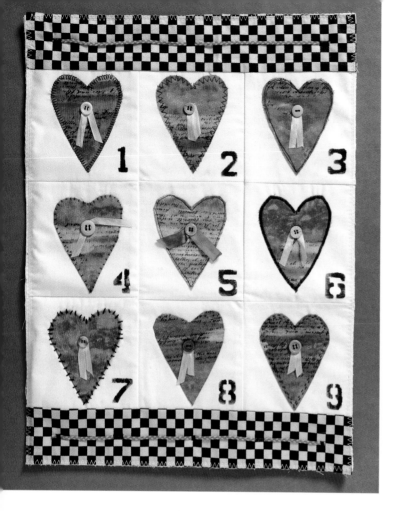

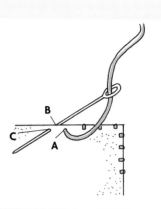

BASIC APPLIQUÉ STITCH

Begin on the back of the fabric. Insert the needle into the small fabric piece approximately 1/16" – 1/8" (1.6–3.2 mm) away from the edge (point A). Reinsert the needle into the background fabric only (point B), directly opposite point A, then bring the tip of the needle out on the small fabric piece (point C) just to the left of point A. Continue working the stitches in this way, one at a time. Try to make all the stitches consistent in length and in distance apart, 1/16" (1.6 mm) for invisible stitching and 1/8" (3.2 mm) for standard appliqué stitching.

Nine Ways to Appliqué

Today's appliqué does not always display the traditional characteristics of turned-under edges and tiny, neat stitches. Variations of machine and hand stitching, and raw and turned edges, add more visual interest to fabric journal pages.

1. Machine blanket stitch on raw edges

2. Machine zigzag stitch on raw edges

3. Multiple rows of machine straight stitching on raw edges

4. Extended-length hand appliqué stitch on turned-under edges

5. Machine top stitch on turned-under edges

6. Machine satin stitch on raw edges

7. Random hand stitch on turned-under edges

8. Traditional hand appliqué stitch on turned-under edges

9. Multiple rows of hand running stitch on raw edges

What Color Thread?

Traditionally, the color of the sewing thread is matched to the color of the appliqué piece, not the background fabric. To make the stitching more visible, choose a high contrast color of thread.

Tools and Supplies for Appliqué

Threads

- 100% cotton for most projects
- 100% rayon for highly visible stitching
- 100% silk for invisible stitching

Adhesives

- Iron-on adhesives, in thin strips on a roll or in flat sheets to be cut to any size
- Fabric glue sticks
- Spray adhesives especially for fabrics, found in quilt supply stores
- Double-stick tape

Freezer paper, found in the supermarket

Needles

- Thin and sharp for invisible stitching, size 10 or 12
- Sharps
- Quilting betweens (very short needles)

Pins

Quilter's pins are too large for most appliqué work. Appliqué pins are very short and small and will not get in the way while sewing. Silk pins, slightly larger than appliqué pins, are another choice.

Small detail scissors

How to Prepare Fabric for Appliqué

1 Decide whether the appliqué piece will have raw or turned-under edges, and determine the shape.

2 For a shape other than square or rectangle, trace the exact size of the shape onto the nonshiny side of a piece of freezer paper. Iron the freezer paper onto the back of the fabric. For turned under edges, add a 1/4" (6 mm) seam allowance to the outside edge of the shape, and cut out the fabric around the seam allowance. For squares and rectangles, cut the fabric 1/2" (1.3 cm) longer and 1/2" (1.3 cm) wider than the desired finished size. For raw edges, cut the fabric piece to the exact size and proceed to step 5.

3 With the freezer paper still in place, press under the seam allowance on the back of the fabric piece. Curves can be cut in 1/8" (3 mm) increments perpendicular to the edge to create a smoother transition. For squares and rectangles, press under 1/4" (6 mm) seam allowance on each side.

4 Gently peel off the freezer paper from the back of the fabric, and press the back and front sides of the appliqué piece with all the edges turned under.

5 Choose a method to hold the appliqué piece in position temporarily while sewing: pins, fabric glue stick, iron-on adhesive, or double-stick tape.

6 The piece is now ready to be applied to the background fabric using the basic appliqué stitch or one of its variations.

A quilt block pattern served as the starting point for this journal page. Quilting in the ditch, or stitching along the seam lines, and diagonal quilting on the roof triangles add extra texture to the page.

Art Quilting

Quilters who have never made a book may not realize how simple the process can be. Take a small art quilt, join several of them together, and you have a fabric art journal. Book artists have much to learn from quilters about putting pages together. First, experiment with piecing different fabrics together to form a whole new cloth piece or page. Second, learn to use background quilting as a way to add texture and visual interest to the pages.

Piecing Fabrics

Joining small strips or squares of fabric together to form a larger piece of whole cloth is the main idea behind making a quilt. Fabric journal artists simply work on a smaller scale. There are hundreds, perhaps even thousands, of different quilt block patterns. Study a block design that appeals to you and explore how the block can be adapted to fit the page design.

When joining fabrics to make cloth for a page, use a $1/4$" (6 mm) seam allowance to join the fabrics. Press as you sew. Create a piece of whole cloth that is several inches or centimeters larger than needed for the page size so that you will have some flexibility in deciding where the seams will fall.

Quilting Backgrounds

When trims and beads seem like too much volume to add to a page, or if time is limited, consider the more subtle approach of a quilted background to define shapes and texture in the fabric.

Quilting can outline an image or shape in a background fabric or an image transfer appliqué, or create a new shape on a simple cloth field. The quilting can be done by hand, or by machine using a walking foot or darning foot, and dropping the feed dogs for free-form design work. In place of stitching, quilting can also be done by hand-tying thread, ribbon, or thin cord through all the layers of fabric.

A good general book on quilting is a useful addition to the journal artist's reference library.

The simple straight stitch, French knot, and stem stitch create the visual texture on this book cover embroidered with pearl cotton no. 5 thread. The corded edge piping is overlaced with the blanket stitch.

Easy Embroidery

Beautiful decorative stitching may be a final embellishment added to fabric journal pages before binding, yet it is hardly an afterthought. Embroidery is a hardworking, extremely versatile craft that completes the composition in ways no other embellishment technique can.

Decades ago, embroidery was carefully executed with neat stitches following precise, controlled patterns. Fabric journal artists can be more casual in their approach, using embroidery to add visual stimulation as well as texture and definition.

Like appliqué, embroidery can be done by hand or machine. Embroidery machines provide options that your grandmother could not have imagined: incredible speed, flawless stitching, and a tremendous repertoire of patterns and alphabets that can be instantly upgraded using a computer and the Internet. Despite these benefits, embroidery machines are no match for the enduring charm of less than perfect hand stitching.

Ways to Use Embroidery in Fabric Journals

- Add background texture with seeding, or tiny stitches worked close together in an irregular pattern.

- Edge or frame appliqué work by embroidering around the borders of the piece.

- Add detail to appliqué by adding a stem to a flower, for example.

- Span the seam where two different fabrics join together, such as with crazy quilting.

- Outline a design or shape printed as part of the fabric pattern.

- Define a new shape on a solid color fabric.

- Add words or text to pages.

Useful reference books with hundreds of embroidery stitch patterns are widely available, but knowledge of only a few basic stitches is enough to get started. Like many other skills, embroidering will improve with practice.

Thread choice plays an important role in the final appearance of embroidery.

- **Six-strand cotton floss** is the most popular choice for embroidery thread for its versatility and wide availability. Its two-ply strands can be easily separated into different thicknesses, and it comes in hundreds of colors.

- **Pearl cotton** is a twisted, single strand thread available in four different weights, with no. 5 the most widely available. It comes in a wide range of colors and has a more textured, rounded appearance than six-strand floss. Pearl cotton is a top choice for blanket-stitch edges on fabric journal pages.

- **Other embroidery threads are available in silk, linen, rayon, and metallics.** These specialty threads can be more difficult to handle because they tend to fray easily. Working with shorter lengths of these more exotic threads will help reduce fraying and tangles.

Tools you will need to incorporate embroidery into fabric journals include embroidery needles in a variety of sizes to accommodate the different types of thread, a small pair of sharp detail scissors for clipping threads, and a thimble.

Easy Embroidery Stitches

STEM STITCH

1 Bring the thread to the front of the fabric on the left end of the design line (point A). Hold down the thread with your left thumb, and insert the needle into the fabric on the design line slightly to the right (point B). Bring the tip of the needle out midway between points A and B (point C). Continue holding down the thread with your thumb as you pull the thread through to set the first stitch.

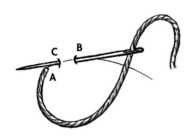

2 Insert the needle into the fabric on the design line slightly to the right of point B. Bring the needle to the front again at point B (in exactly the same hole). Hold the thread down with your left thumb and pull the thread through to set the second stitch. Continue working the embroidery in this way. Try to make all the stitches about 1/8" (3 mm) in length.

To tie off, take the needle to the back at the end of the design line. Anchor the thread with three or four small loop knots.

STRAIGHT STITCH OR SEED STITCH

1 Bring the needle to the front of the fabric (point A).

2 Insert the needle back into the fabric (point B) for the desired stitch length, and then bring it out at the beginning of the next stitch (point C).

To tie off, take the needle to the back on the last stitch. Anchor the thread with three or four small loop knots.

Straight stitches can be worked uniformly or irregularly as seed stitches, depending upon the effect you wish to achieve. It is best to keep them short in length and resting firmly against the background fabric; they tend to snag when they are too long or too loose.

Use the straight stitch to create free-form cross-stitches by crossing the exit stitch (point C) over the previous stitch (connecting points A and B) before entering the fabric again.

BACK STITCH

1 Bring the thread to the front of the fabric, a short distance from the right end of the design line (point A).

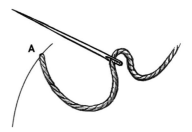

2 Insert the needle into the fabric at the end of the design line (point B). Bring the tip of the needle out on the design line to the left of point A (point C). Pull the thread through to set the first stitch.

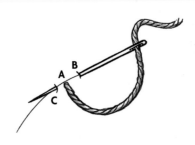

3 Reinsert the needle into the fabric at point A (in exactly the same hole). Bring the tip of the needle out on the design line to the left of point C (point D). Pull the thread through to set the second stitch. Continue working the embroidery in this way. Try to make all the stitches about 1/16" (less than 2 mm) in length.

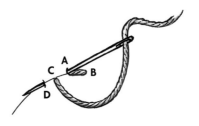

BUTTONHOLE STITCH

1 Bring the needle to the front of the fabric. Holding the thread down with your left thumb, insert the needle into the fabric at point A and come back out at point B. Still holding the thread down with your thumb, pull the needle through the fabric and over the working thread.

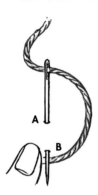

2 Repeat the step 1 motion. The stitches in the illustration are slightly separated to clarify the technique, but you should work yours close together so that no background fabric shows through.

To tie off, take the needle to the back on the last stitch at the end of the design line. Anchor the thread with three or four small loop knots.

FRENCH KNOT

1 Bring the needle to the front of the fabric where the knot will be. Hold the thread taut between your left thumb and index finger approximately 1" (2.5 cm) away from the fabric.

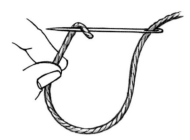

2 Using your left hand, wrap the thread once around the needle.

3 Hold the thread taut again, and insert the needle into the fabric one or two threads away from the starting point. Push the needle to the back of the fabric, while holding the thread down with your left thumb. Release your thumb as you pull the thread through to the back to set the knot.

Your completed French knot should resemble a "Granny's bun" hairstyle. For bolder French knots, wrap the thread three times instead of once, in step 2.

Eyelets & Other Hardware

Colorful metal eyelets are small but hardworking embellishments that serve many useful functions in constructing fabric art journals. An eyelet permanently defines and maintains the openings cut into cloth. Its metal casing provides extra strength and stability to the opening, and it protects the raw edges of the fabric from fraying.

Eyelets function equally well on fabric and paper. Paper eyelets offer more choices in color, finish, and stem length, and will work well in fabrics that are not too bulky. Standard paper eyelets appear much smaller than their fabric counterparts, even though both are labeled as $\frac{1}{8}$" (3 mm) in size.

Eyelets Can be Used for Many Purposes

- Joining pages together. Fabric art journals with flat-panel pages can be attached at the sides by setting eyelets and threading colorful cord or other decorative fiber through the holes.
- Reinforcing openings that are functional or purely decorative.
- Attaching items to the page, such as beads on jump rings, decorative fibers, and other embellishments.
- Attaching labels, nameplates, and letters to the page, in place of using buttons or beads.

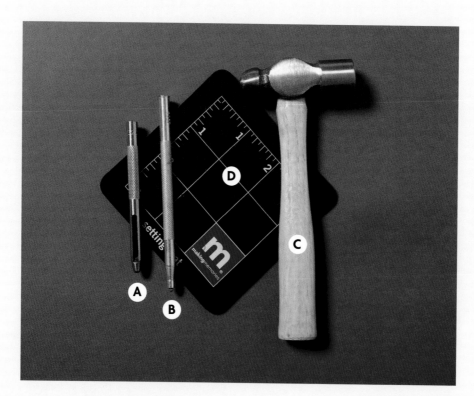

TOOLS

Tools needed to set an eyelet:

- HOLLOW HOLE PUNCH (**A**)
- EYELET SETTER TOOL (**B**)
- SMALL HAMMER (**C**)
- SETTING MAT (optional) (**D**)

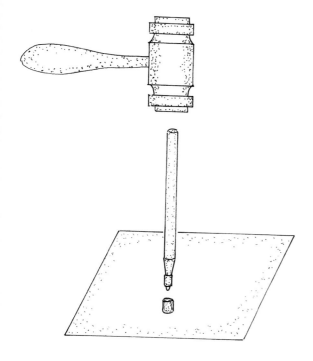

How to Attach an Eyelet with a Punch, Setter, and Hammer

SETTING AN EYELET IS A THREE-STEP PROCESS:

1 Punch a hole in the fabric that is the same size as the eyelet stem.

2 Insert the eyelet stem into the punched hole with the finished end of the eyelet on the right side of the fabric. Place the front side of the fabric face down on the setting mat or work surface with the stem facing up.

3 Place the point tip of the eyelet setter into the stem of the eyelet, holding the setter straight. Use a hammer to tap the end of the eyelet setter very firmly once or twice to fold back the eyelet stem. Remove the setter and tap directly on the eyelet rim, moving in a circular motion around the edges.

How to Make an Eyelet by Hand Sewing

Eyelets can be hand sewn without a metal rim, much like a round buttonhole. Punch or cut a hole of the desired size into the cloth. Stitch around the outline of the hole with the running stitch to define the area. Use the buttonhole stitch to bind the raw fabric edges around the opening.

How to Set an Eyelet with Eyelet Pliers

Eyelet pliers are sold in the notions department of fabric stores. Most use a two-step process to set an eyelet, but both functions are performed with the same tool.

1 Punch the hole and push the eyelet into the fabric.

2 Insert the pliers into the eyelet stem and apply pressure to the handles, rolling back the stem of the eyelet into the fabric.

Instructions for using these tools vary by manufacturer, so follow the directions provided with the tool.

TIPS FOR SETTING EYELETS

• • • • •

- Always set an eyelet in fabric that is reinforced with interfacing, or that has at least two layers of cloth. The eyelet's metal rim must have enough material to grip to be properly set.

- After punching the hole and before inserting the eyelet stem, be sure to remove any cloth or stray threads from the opening. Use detail scissors to snip away excess not removed by the punch. However, do not enlarge the hole during this process or it may become too big to securely hold the eyelet.

Other Hardware Choices

More hardware attachment options for fabric journals can be found in scrapbook supply stores. The notions department of the fabric store will yield still more hardware options.

- **Brads** are decorative eyelets with solid heads. They are set in the same way but do not provide the opening for other materials to pass through.

- **Grommets** are part of the eyelet family. They tend to be larger and are used when an industrial-strength reinforcement is needed. Some grommets have two parts, a front and a back, and use setters that are typically sold with the grommets, although some tools will set both eyelets and grommets.

- **Dugaree buttons** and **bachelor buttons** are no-sew options for achieving the hardware look without the tools. These attachments have two parts, the decorative front and a thumb tack–style back. The front is positioned on the right side of of the fabric and the tack is pushed in from the back. Light tapping on the tack with a hammer helps secure the connection.

Buttons

Buttons are the secret weapon in the fabric book artist's arsenal. Nothing in the paper book arts world can quite compare to the versatility of this tiny but powerful embellishment. Buttons can stand alone or as a group, they can be functional, or they can be simply objects of beauty. These little extras can add volumes of visual and tactile interest to fabric books.

A trip to the fabric or button store to choose buttons can be almost as daunting as choosing a wallpaper pattern, so it's best to have a plan in mind before you start. The thrill of the hunt for the perfect button can become a fun task when making a fabric art journal. Novelty and themed button collections have proliferated in recent years.

Buttons create the most interest when they make a meaningful or creative contribution to the story or to the visual design of the page. They can also function as fabric journal closures when combined with a buttonhole or cord wrap. Consider these uses for buttons as design elements in cloth books.

Types of Button Embellishments

- **One Great Button.** This fabulous button is so compelling, and so perfect, that it is the only button needed on the page. You'll know it right away when you find it.

- **Repeat Pattern Buttons.** Many buttons of the same size, shape, or color can fill a page quickly with

pattern, texture and color. Try alternating buttons with other elements, such as fabric appliqué squares or tied-off silk ribbons.

- **Buttons as Art Starters.** Select a simple, large button and use it as the centerpiece of a design. Layer colorful fabric beneath the button, then sew all the layers together with thread in a contrasting color.

- **Buttons as Body Parts.** Buttons make colorful fingernails and rings on large hands, heads on dolls, people, or animal figures, as well as other body parts.

- **Buttons as Frames.** Surround an image transfer with a selection of buttons for a picture-frame effect.

- **Buttons as Anchors.** Affix labels, individual letters, blocks of text, and fabric shapes, using buttons as corner anchors.

- **Buttons as Fillers.** Cover otherwise unadorned areas of a page with a variety of buttons to add texture and color interest. For example, the roof of a house can be fashioned from rows of small buttons.

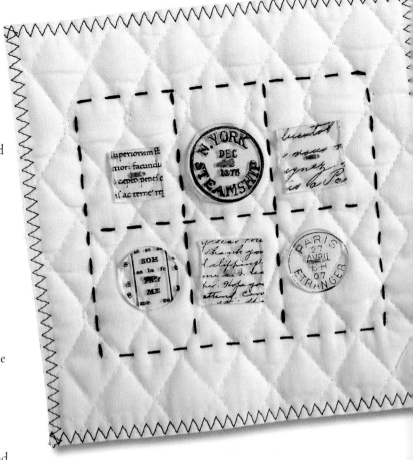

Custom-Made Buttons

Ready-made buttons can be found everywhere: at craft stores, flea markets, thrift stores, tag sales, dollar stores, and quilt, fabric, and yarn shops. Some of the best button finds come from the prized jar of a favorite relative's lifetime collection. Even with so many button choices, there will still be times when a special project calls for a custom button. Try these simple techniques to fashion one-of-a-kind creations for your work.

Acrylic Buttons

Clear acrylic buttons come in many sizes and shapes, and serve as an ideal surface for layered collage effects. Add images and text to the surfaces with rubber stamp images and solvent-based inks that are specially formulated to work on nonporous materials. Both the top and the bottom surfaces of a clear button can be used for design. Stamp text images or letters on the top surface; apply contrasting designs to the bottom surface using stamps or paper collage for a multilayered effect. Decorative paper can be glued to the back of the acrylic button using clear acrylic mounting tape or a clear dimensional adhesive.

This collection of clear acrylic buttons (see photograph, top) was created with a variety of rubber stamp images stamped on the top surface with solvent inks. To be readable, words and letters must be stamped on only the top surface of a clear button.

After stamping the top surface, a layer of decorative paper was added to the bottom surface of these buttons, creating a mini-collage piece, with depth and color (see photograph, far right).

ACRYLIC BUTTON TIP

· · · · ·

To control the image position on acrylic buttons, use a reverse inking process. Apply ink to the rubber stamp image, then place it inked-side up on the work surface. Gently lower the button onto the desired area of the design and press lightly until the ink transfers to the acrylic surface. Remove the button carefully and allow the ink to thoroughly dry.

Fabric-Covered Buttons

Easy-to-use kits for covering buttons with fabric can be found in the notions department of fabric stores. Some self-covering button forms have a rounded, dome-like surface, while others are flat; both styles come in many sizes. Buttons covered with novelty fabric prints make lively three-dimensional additions to your book pages.

Hand-Painted Buttons

Flat wooden shapes and colorful acrylic paint can be combined to create unique custom buttons. The woodcrafting section of the craft store typically stocks several styles and sizes of blank round disks,

These button-head gals (below) have lots of personality and dimension. Domed forms were covered with novelty cloth that was carefully cut around the face area of the glamour girl design fabric. The bodies were cut from children's novelty cloth and appliquéd to the background. The perfect cat novelty button was just the right size to complete this fabric collage piece.

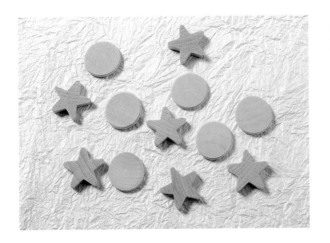

TIP

• • • • •

If you are making more than one wooden button at a time, create a paper or card-stock template for the hole positions. It will save you time measuring each button individually, and the finished buttons will look more uniform.

but look for other shapes, too, including hearts, stars, and flowers as candidates for hand-painted buttons. Use a hand drill with a ⅟₁₆" (1.6 mm) or ⅟₃₂" (2.4 mm) bit to make holes in the wood for sewing, then lightly sand the surface of the wood blank to prepare it for painting. Apply two base coats of acrylic paint to all sides of the blank—don't forget the edges—then add special shading or painted designs to the top surface and the sides. Use rubber stamp alphabets to create letter buttons. When the paint is completely dry, apply one or two coats of a clear acrylic sealant, then use very fine steel wool to give the surface a smooth finish.

These hand-painted letter buttons (below) have holes drilled near the edge, rather than in the center, so that the thread does not detract from the visual impact of the letterforms.

TIPS FOR ATTACHING BUTTONS

• • • • •

• Sew on buttons with strong craft and button thread, going through the holes at least five or six times. Buttons receive a lot of handling, so attach them firmly.

• Never sew a button to a single layer of fabric. Add additional reinforcement such as batting or interfacing behind the decorative fabric layer to support the sewing.

• If the button will be used functionally, as in a buttonhole or other closure, add a thread shank or small additional button spacer between the button and the back ground fabric.

• Try variety in sewing on buttons. Just because the holes are in the center of the button doesn't mean the thread must be sewn between the holes. Loop the thread around the outside edges of the button instead for a different look.

• If practical, sew on buttons near the end of the page embellishment process. Large buttons can get in the way of pressing or machine sewing, so do those tasks first.

• Never iron buttons. They can melt, crack, or discolor from the heat, steam, or weight of the iron.

Fancy Edges

There are many options for elaborately finishing the page and cover edges of fabric journals. Although these techniques will require more time to complete than a basic edge finish, they add much more pizzazz to the final project.

Bias Tape

Bias tape can be used to encase the raw edges of the page, adding color contrast at the same time. The tape lies completely flat and can be neatly mitered at the corners for a clean look. It can also be used as a base for making corded binding and beaded edges. Bias tape can be purchased in basic colors at the fabric store, and in a variety of prints and patterns at quilt supply stores as quilt binding. You can also make your own bias tape from any fabric with a bias tape maker and an iron.

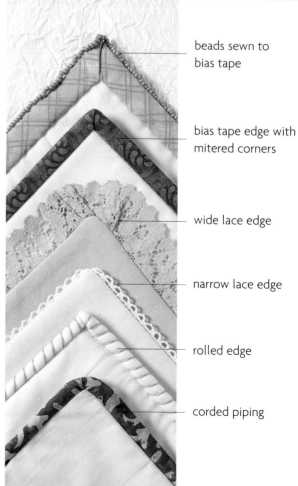

beads sewn to bias tape

bias tape edge with mitered corners

wide lace edge

narrow lace edge

rolled edge

corded piping

How to Attach Bias Tape with Mitered Corners

The seam allowance is ¹⁄₂" (1.3 cm) and the bias tape is 2" (5.1 cm) wide, folded to 1" (2.5 cm).

1 Cut a length of bias tape that is a few inches longer than needed for the project. Turn under ¹⁄₂" (1.3 cm) on the starting short end of the tape. Pin the tape to the top edge of the fabric, right sides together. Straight stitch from the starting end of the tape, stopping ¹⁄₂" (1.3 cm) away from the corner.

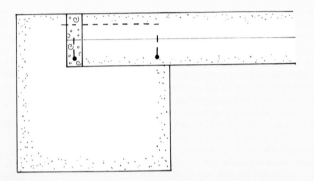

2 Fold up the bias tape at the corner, creating a 45° angle. Pin the angle in place.

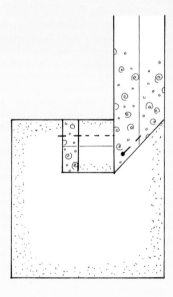

3 Fold down the bias tape, covering the pinned angle. Straight stitch from the corner, stopping ¹⁄₂" (1.3 cm) away from the next corner.

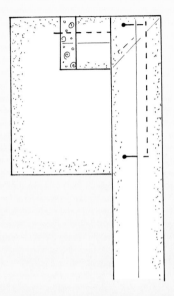

4 Repeat steps 2 and 3 until all four corners have been sewn.

5 Overlap the two ends of the bias tape by about 1" (2.5 cm). Cut away the excess bias tape and pin the loose end in place. Straight stitch the remaining edge and the overlapped tape ends.

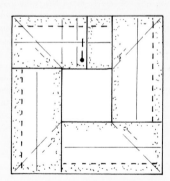

6 Fold back the bias tape along the seam line, turning the unsewn edge of the tape to the back of the fabric. Use your fingers to adjust the miter fold at each corner.

7 On the back, fold each corner in turn to form a miter and pin in place. Press.

8 Turn under the bias tape's raw edge ½" (1.3 cm) and press. Hand stitch the bias tape's edge to the back of the fabric. Take a few stitches at each corner to join the miter folds together.

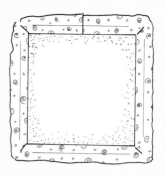
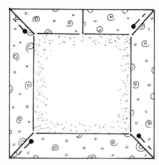
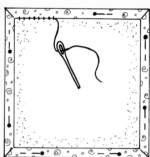

Corded Piping

Corded piping provides a soft, dimensional finish to a cover or page edge. It is made by enclosing a continuous piece of cord inside a strip of bias tape. The cord is available in several different widths, and the tape must be wide enough both to enclose the cord and to provide a base to stitch to the background fabric.

Corded piping can also be purchased at the fabric or upholstery store, along with braided cord trims. Follow the procedure for attaching corded piping when sewing braided trim to background fabric.

Rolled Edge

Similar in appearance to corded piping but much easier to make, the rolled edge adds lots of extra dimension to the page edge. The rounded edge is created by rolling down the fabric and securing it with the whip stitch, sewn with embroidery floss. This finish requires additional seam allowance (¼" to ½" [0.6–1.3 cm] more) beyond the standard ½" (1.3 cm) edge indicated for many of the projects in this book.

Lace

Lace can be added to journal page edges before the page spreads are joined into signatures. For narrow lace, pin the inner edge of the lace just outside the page seam line and baste in place before sewing the final seams.

To sew wider lace, match the inner edge of the lace with the raw edge of the background fabric on a page spread, right sides together. At the corners, clip around the curves or add a few extra tucks of lace on each side of the corner to avoid bunching. Baste in place. Add the second page spread on top, right side facing in, and stitch around the outside seam allowance, leaving an open seam area at the bottom to turn the pages right side out. Slip stitch the open area closed by hand.

Beads

Beads can be sewn onto an enclosed seam edge or onto bias tape using the Three-Bead Back Stitch (see page 58). When sewing beads to the page, take into account the extra weight they will add to the fabric, and reinforce the inside of the pages accordingly.

How to Sew Corded Piping

Sewing corded piping is a two-step process, and is much faster to complete on a sewing machine. Start with equal lengths of cord and bias tape that are several inches longer than needed for the project.

1 To encase the cord, place the cord in the fold of the bias tape, then pin the long edges of the tape together. Straight stitch across the approximate center of the folded bias tape, loosely encasing the cord.

2 To attach the piping, pin the corded piping to the background fabric, matching the raw edges. Clip ¼" (6 mm) increments around the corners and overlap the two short ends of the tape about 1" (2.5 cm). Straight stitch the bias tape to the background fabric about ¼" (6 mm) away from the first row of stitching, closer to the encased cord. Use the zipper foot on the sewing machine for a very close stitch.

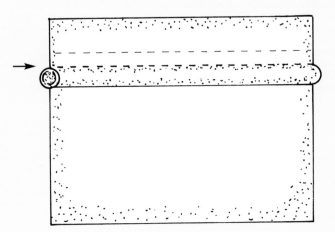

How to Make a Rolled Edge

1 Roll down the edge of the fabric at least twice. Make the roll fairly tight, and hold it in place with your hand, because the fabric will be too thick to use pins.

2 Whip stitch the fabric roll along the edges at regular intervals, ⅛" (3 mm) or ¼" (6 mm) apart, and continue until all the edges are sewn down.

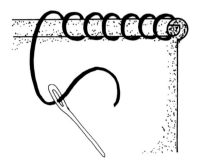

TIPS FOR MAKING ROLLED EDGES

• Trim away the inner layers of fabric and batting or interfacing about ¼" (6 mm). This reduces some fabric bulk in the rolling process, making it easier to turn in the raw edges.

• Miter cut the page batting or interfacing layer at the corners to reduce bulk and allow a smooth transition of the two edges.

Fancy Closures

(A)

(B)

(C)

(A) D-rings and printed twill tape form an adjustable closure on this flower journal. (B) The bead and bead loop create an elegant closure. (C) This flap closure is secured with a buttonhole and a button, but a Velcro dot would work just as well.

A special closure on your fabric art journal can provide a finishing touch, or serve the useful purpose of keeping the contents under control. Closures can be incorporated into the journal's structural design or added as an afterthought. Try one of these idea-starters to help create a unique solution to overstuffed journal pages.

Simple Endings

- **Ribbon.** Beautiful ribbons can be sewn into the seam allowance and edge finishes of a fabric journal, then tied together to contain the pages. Choose sturdy, woven ribbons such as grosgrain or satin. Silk ribbons, while striking in color, do not hold up well to repeated use and are better suited for embellishment than for functional work.

- **Twill Tape and D-rings.** A length of twill tape and a couple of metal D-rings can complete a stylish closure that is both adjustable and trendy. Choose twill tape that is the same width as the flat side of the D-ring. Cut the tape about 6" (15.2 cm) longer than the length needed to reach completely around the journal. Insert one end of the twill tape through the flat ends of both D-rings, then wrap it around to the back of the tape, overlapping 1" (2.5 cm), or more for large rings. Stitch the overlapped ends together close to the rings to secure them. To close, insert the loose end of the twill tape through the rounded ends of both D-rings, then double back the tape end through one D-ring only and pull to tighten. The twill tape can be sewn to the back of the journal with a few tacking stitches.

- **Belt Buckles.** Purchase a fancy or utilitarian belt buckle clasp and thread it with fabric, twill tape, ribbon, or braided trim to fashion a substantial looking closure. If the buckle has a prong in the middle, punch holes in the fabric or ribbon and set eyelets in the holes.

- **Backpack Hardware.** Making tote bags and backpacks is now a popular craft; as a result, there are many interesting clasps and connectors available in industrial plastic or painted metal. Combine this hardware with flat webbing, twill tape, or cording to create a closure.

- **Fabric Frogs.** Looped and knotted decorative cord makes a lovely closure with an Asian feel. Called fabric frogs, these connections can be purchased already made, or make your own knot and loop closures using decorative satin cording. A good book on decorative knots, or knot-making templates from the notions department, will provide guidance on how to create this closure.

Advance Planning Required

- **Flap Closure.** An extension of the journal's back cover can wrap around the fore edge and connect with the front cover, using a Velcro tab. For stability, the flap should be sewn securely to the back cover or cut as part of the entire cloth of the back cover.

- **Sewn-on Tapes.** Fabric journals based on the tape-bound journal model can extend one or more of the binding tapes to form a closure.

- **Buttonholes.** Buttonholes can be created by hand or by machine and set into flap closures.

- **Button and Bead Loop Closure.** Tiny round seed beads and a single beautiful button can work together to form a stunning closure. Determine the position of the large button on the front cover and attach it. On the back cover's fore edge, attach a needle threaded with strong beading cord or thread. String the beads onto the thread until the cord can comfortably loop around the attached button and return to the back cover's fore edge, plus an extra 1/2" (1.3 cm) to set and remove the loop during use. Tie off the bead string securely. As an option in place of strung beads, use a simple satin or cotton cord.

Beads

Beads are nearly as versatile as buttons when it comes to enlivening a page or cover. They add instant color and texture, and they can bring functional closures and stitching to life by adding dimension. Like their button cousins, beads come in a tremendous number of possibilities for size, shape, and color, but they have a key distinguishing feature—beads can be attached to the page invisibly. A good selection of beads is an excellent addition to the fabric journal artist's supply pantry.

Here are some ways to include beads in fabric art journals.

- Give focus to the page design with a single beautiful bead or a fun novelty bead.

- Anchor a closure with a substantial bead in place of a button for a buttonhole closure, or use wired or strung beads to create a closure loop for a large bead or button.

- Add words to the page using alphabet beads, or create letterforms by stringing small beads together and sewing them to the background.

- Create visual texture. Small beads combine well with seed stitch embroidery to create a pleasing textural contrast on a fabric background.

- Embellish page edges. Single beads placed intermittently, or small beads attached in a continuous strand, add an elegant look to fabric. Elaborate fringe beading can add movement and color.

- Frame or outline other art on the page with small rows of seed beads. They can be sewn around an image transfer or appliqué piece.

- Slide beads onto binding threads, cords, tapes, and ribbons to enhance the binding, or add beads to decorative fibers for bookmarks and other attached embellishments. Beads with large holes are needed for thicker fibers and ribbons.

TIPS FOR ATTACHING BEADS

· · · · ·

- Sew beads on securely. Start on the reverse side of the fabric, and go through the bead hole several times with a double thickness of thread. Finish on the back with a knot.

- If you are sewing on more than one bead to a large fabric area using the same thread, tie a knot on the back after each bead is attached.

- Always sew beads to fabric with a support layer attached.

- For straight or looped strands of beads, use very strong thread. This type of embellishment may catch on other dimensional items as the journal pages are handled, so the strands should be securely anchored.

- Don't iron beads. They can melt, discolor, or crack from the heat and weight of the iron. Complete all the fabric pressing first before adding beads, or iron carefully around them.

Embellishing with Small Beads

Tiny beads take extra patience and time to handle and attach to fabric pages, but they are well worth the added effort.

- **Seed beads** are the smallest beads, often sold by weight in clear tubes.

- **Rocailles,** which include the seed bead family, are small round beads that come in a range of sizes from 16/0, the smallest, to 1/0, the largest. The 6/0 size bead, also called an E bead, is a popular choice with fabric and embroidery artists.

- **Bugles** are small tube beads, also available in a range of sizes based on length, from 1/2 (the shortest) to 5 (the longest). The hole diameter of a bugle bead is usually equal to the diameter of a seed bead.

Fringe Beads

Exotic fringe beads are a popular embellishment for clothing and home decorating items, and they add visual excitement to the edge of a fabric journal page. Fringe beads are sold prepackaged or by the yard in fabric and upholstery supply stores. They come attached to a small strip of ribbon or tape that is sewn into the seam area of the fabric piece or appliquéd to the background fabric.

TIPS FOR WORKING WITH TINY BEADS

· · · · ·

- Thin beading needles used to string tiny beads are too flexible and blunt to pierce multiple layers of fabric. Seed beads and other small rocailles can be sewn with appliqué and between needles, size 10, which are strong enough to sew through multiple layers of fabric.

- Gold-eye needles are easier to thread than their plain counterparts.

- A small, table model needle threader speeds up the threading process.

- Pick up seed beads easily by dipping the needle tip into the bead container until the desired number of beads have transferred to the shaft.

- Attach rows or solid areas of seed beads to fabric using the Three-Bead Back Stitch (see page 58).

- Tiny beads can also be attached using a two-step process. First, string the beads together with a beading needle and fine silk thread. Next, attach the strand of beads to the fabric background with a couching stitch (described in the Trims section; see page 59).

The Three-Bead Back Stitch

This stitch can be used to attach seed beads along a design line (such as a letterform or shape), to outline another shape, or to cover an area of fabric with solid beads. When following a specific line, first draw the design on the fabric background with chalk or a very fine line pencil.

1 Begin with the threaded needle on the back of the fabric. Push the needle tip through the fabric at the beginning point of the design line. Pick up three beads on the needle tip.

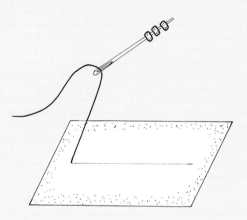

2 Slide the beads onto the thread. Push the needle tip back through the fabric at the point on the design line where the beads end. Pull the thread taut.

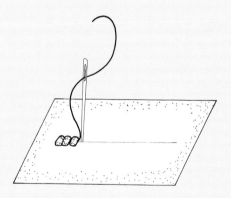

3 Push the needle through to the front of the fabric again, coming up between the second and third bead.

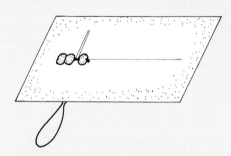

4 Enter the hole of the third bead and pull the thread through, pick up three more beads and reenter the fabric on the design line where the beads end. Repeat this step until the design is completed.

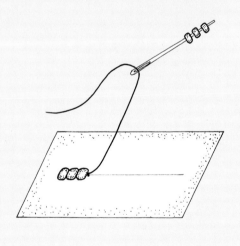

Lining Up Beads in Even Rows

The alignment of beads sewn in short rows can be improved by first sewing on the individual beads, then reentering the entire row with one continuous thread. Use this technique to straighten rows of words composed with alphabet beads.

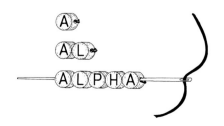

Trims

Fabric journal pages embellished with beautiful trimmings provide a visual feast for the eyes, adding color, definition, and texture to the surface. Trims can be used to encircle a page, to define an area, or to frame an image, and can also be cleverly used to conceal cutting or sewing errors on an otherwise perfect piece.

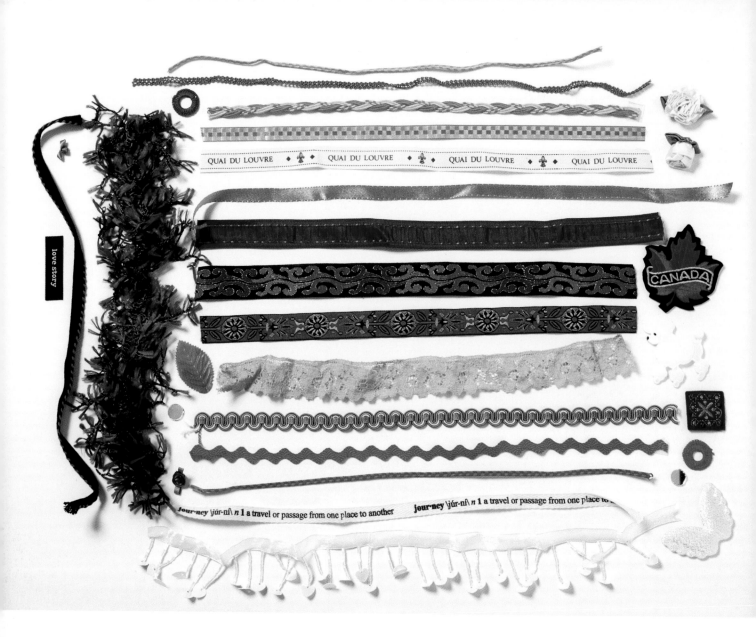

Types of Trims

A trip to the fabric store's trimming department is nearly as daunting as a button hunt. Thousands of choices abound. Most trims are sold by the yard; a few, such as rickrack, are prepackaged. These broad categories group the types of trims available.

Flat Trims

This category includes ribbons, cords, silk and Russian braids, rickrack, beading and sequin strips, and European embroidered tapes. Many of these can be attached with machine sewing, although some (such as beading strips) may require the use of a special beading foot attachment. Some can even be glued to the page using good-quality fabric glue.

Open Trims

This group includes lace, beaded lace, feathers, intertwined decorative cord trims, and fringe. Unless the trim has a sewing tape or edge attached, it will be sewn on by hand.

Object Trims

This category includes dimensional items such as tassels, sticks, found objects, ribbon flowers, leaves, shisha mirrors, metal tags, and any other items you may wish to attach. These items are sewn on by hand or can be wired onto the page for extra security or visual effect.

How to Attach Trims

A few basic hand and machine stitches are all that are needed to attach trims. The stitching can be made nearly invisible by using small stitches and thread to match the trim or the background fabric color, or it can become an aesthetic part of the trim through stitching that stands out in size or thread color.

MACHINE OR HAND STRAIGHT STITCH

Use this stitch to attach ribbons, flat cords, braids, rickrack, and flat embroidered tapes. Lace trims and fringe with sewing tapes attached can be straight stitched. Russian braid has a center groove or ditch where the stitching can be hidden.

MACHINE ZIGZAG STITCH

This stitch can add some visual punch to the trim attachment and is used for ribbon, flat cords, rickrack, and the edges of flat embroidered tapes. For narrow flat trims, adjust the width of the stitch so that it completely spans the width of the trim without piercing it.

TACKING

This hand or machine stitch is used when only a few critical stitches are needed here and there to secure the trim. Open trims and small objects such as ribbon flowers are good candidates for tacking.

WIRING

When thread seems too fragile to secure substantial looking items to the page, consider the use of fine gauge (24 or 28) wire to do the sewing. Push the wire through the fabric from the back, leaving a small tail about 2" (5.1 cm) long. Wrap the wire around the item several times and reinsert the wire into the fabric. Twist the two wire ends together on the back and clip away the excess. The background fabric should have a layer of interfacing or batting to help support the wire.

COUCHING

This hand stitch (below left) can hold a narrow flat trim in place and direct its flow and position on the page. Couching is not suitable for wide flat trims, because the long stitches can be caught or snagged by other items on the page.

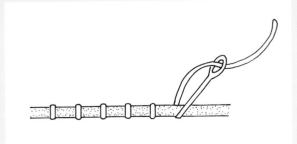

The slender metallic trim on this fabric journal page was attached by couching with thread in a contrasting color. The small-scale braided trim around the page edges used the procedure for corded piping.

Chapter Three

FABRIC BOOK PROJECTS

Your **TOOL KIT** *is packed, you know where you want to go, and here are your* **ROAD MAPS.**

The projects in this section provide complete how-to instructions on making a variety of fabric art journals. They are grouped by level of skill required to complete the project—simple, intermediate, and advanced—to help you decide which projects to tackle first. Some of the journals have additional patterns or templates associated with their construction, so be sure to check the Templates section for more information, if needed.

Many of these projects are based on traditional book-binding structures, such as the Coptic-Bound and French-Stitch Journals, and artists who have made these bindings in paper before will find the fabric version very familiar. Art quilters who have never made a book may find they want to try a traditional paper book binding once they have completed a journal in fabric.

When I experiment with a new book binding in paper or fabric, I almost always make a model first. For fabric journals, I like to work with unbleached muslin using a contrasting thread color. It's a good practice tool, and allows me to work out all the problems and details of the project before I invest many hours in embellishing pages or cutting into "precious" fabric that I may not be able to replace easily. A model takes a small fraction of the time you'll invest in making the final project, at very little cost, and will help improve your skill level at the same time.

SIMPLE BINDINGS

Plain muslin is the background, but a
rainbow of color from buttons and silk
ribbons brings this basic journal to life.

Embellishment Idea

For a soft pastel or vintage look, tea-
dye the muslin before cutting it to size.
(See page 22 for more on tea dyeing.)

Muslin Journal

This is a good first fabric book project, because it uses simple materials and sewing techniques. It can be created as a blank journal, with embellishments added to the pages later, or the pages can be completely decorated before sewing the book together. This book has three signatures (twelve individual pages total) plus a cover that is slightly larger than the pages.

MATERIALS

Note: These fabric sizes make the largest book. Adapt the size of your book as desired by following the chart provided.

FOR THE INSIDE PAGES

- 6 PIECES SINGLE THICKNESS COTTON MUSLIN, 8½" × 16" (21.6 × 40.6 cm)
- 3 PIECES LOW-LOFT COTTON BATTING, 8½" × 16" (21.6 × 40.6 cm)

FOR THE COVER

- 1 PIECE QUILTED MUSLIN, 9" × 19" (22.9 × 48.3 cm)
- 1 PIECE SINGLE THICKNESS MUSLIN, 9" × 19" (22.9 × 48.3 cm)
- 1 PIECE COTTON BATTING, 9" × 19" (22.9 × 48.3 cm)
- 100% COTTON SEWING THREAD

TOOLS

- ROTARY CUTTER
- QUILTER'S RULER
- CUTTING MAT
- SCISSORS
- CHALK MARKING PENCILS IN SEVERAL COLORS
- STRAIGHT PINS
- HAND-SEWING NEEDLES
- SEWING MACHINE (OPTIONAL)
- STEAM IRON
- PRESSING SURFACE

SIZE VARIATIONS	LARGE JOURNAL	MEDIUM JOURNAL	SMALL JOURNAL
Finished page size:	7½" (19.0 cm) square	6" (15.2 cm) square	4" (10.2 cm) square
Cut materials size:			
• TEXT PAGES	8½" x 16" (21.6 x 40.6 cm)	7" x 13" (17.8 x 33.0 cm)	5" x 9" (12.7 x 22.9 cm)
• COVER	9" x 19" (22.9 x 48.3 cm)	7½" x 16" (19.0 x 40.6 cm)	5½" x 11" (14.0 x 27.9 cm)

Rows of buttons in a variety of sizes and colors are sewn to the edge of each page.

SEWING AND CONSTRUCTION TIPS

• • • • •

- Cutting the fabric larger than needed will help create neater edges and more accurate sizing. Fabrics can stretch and shift during sewing and handling. Start with larger fabric pieces, sew the main seam lines, then trim the excess fabric from all the layers at one time for a clean, accurate edge.

- Zigzag stitch along the edges, or finish the edges shortly after cutting them to help prevent fraying or stretching.

- Chalk lines applied to fabric wash away when an item is laundered. Because most fabric books will never be machine washed, the chalk lines should be removed with a damp sponge.

- When sewing a signature to the cover, make a few extra backstitches at the beginning and end points to strengthen and stabilize the book's construction.

Making the Inside Pages

1 CREATE A PAGE "SANDWICH"

Place one piece of the inside page muslin face down on the work surface. Layer one piece of the cotton batting, then layer another piece of the muslin, facing up. Align the edges of the three pieces as closely as possible. On the top layer, mark the vertical center with a chalk marking pencil. Sew a straight or running stitch along the chalk line.

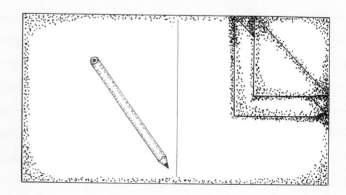

2 SEW THE OUTSIDE EDGES

Measure 7½" (19.1 cm) away from each side of the sewn vertical line and mark with a chalk pencil. Mark horizontal lines at the top and bottom edges, 7½" (19.1 cm) apart (A). Pin the layers of fabric together and sew a straight or running stitch along the chalk lines (B).

3 TRIM AND FINISH THE OUTSIDE EDGES

Use the rotary cutter and the quilter's ruler to trim the excess fabric on each edge, ¼" (6 mm) from the stitching (A). Sew the outside edges together on all four edges using a zigzag, blanket, or decorative stitch, or use pinking shears to trim the fabric close to the sewing edge (B). Press the fabric. Create three complete signatures using this procedure.

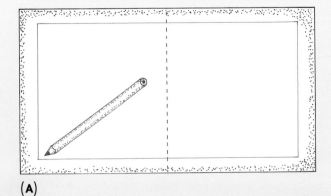

(A)

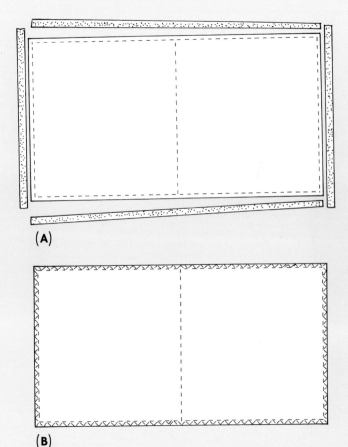

(A)

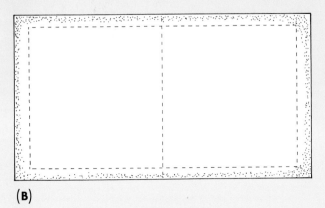

(B)

(B)

Making the Cover

4 CREATE THE COVER "SANDWICH"

Place the piece of quilted muslin face down. Layer the piece of cotton batting, then place the single piece of muslin face up on the top. Align the edges of the three pieces as closely as possible. Mark the center vertical line with a chalk pencil, but do not sew it yet. Draw a second vertical chalk line ½" (1.3 cm) away from the center on the left side, and draw a third vertical chalk line ½" (1.3 cm) away from the center on the right side. These lines will serve as sewing guides for adding the three signatures later.

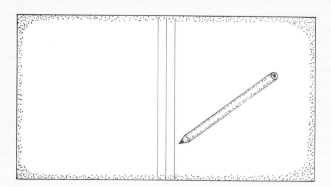

5 SEW THE OUTSIDE EDGES

Create guidelines for sewing the outside edges of the cover. Use the quilter's ruler to mark horizontal guidelines for the height of the book, 8" (20.3 cm) tall. Position the guidelines so that the excess fabric at the top and bottom edges measures about ½" (1.3 cm). Mark with a chalk pencil. Next, create the sewing guidelines for the length of the cover. Use the left vertical guideline as the starting point, and measure 8" (20.3 cm) to the left. Mark with the chalk pencil. Use the right vertical guideline and measure 8" (20.3 cm) to the right, marking with the chalk pencil. Sew along the guidelines, using a straight or running stitch.

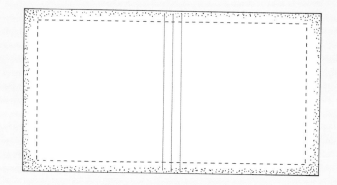

6 TRIM AND FINISH THE OUTSIDE EDGES

Use the cutter and ruler to trim the excess fabric on the edges, ¼" (6 mm) from the stitching. Sew the outside edges together using a zigzag, blanket, or a decorative stitch. Press the fabric.

Binding the Book

The signatures can now be sewn to the cover. Decide on the order of the pages, fold each signature in half on the center stitching line, and stack them in the order they will appear in the finished book.

7   START IN THE MIDDLE

Take the middle signature from the stack and open it up to the center. Align the stitched centerline of the signature with the center chalk guideline on the inside cover. Center the signature at the top and bottom, then pin it to the cover. On top of the existing center line stitching, sew through all the layers of fabric using a straight or running stitch.

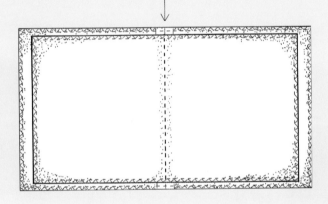

8   SEW THE END SIGNATURE

Flip the middle signature pages to the left side. Take the bottom signature from the stack, open it up, and align the stitched centerline with the right chalk guideline. Center the signature at the top and bottom, pin it in place, and sew it to the cover.

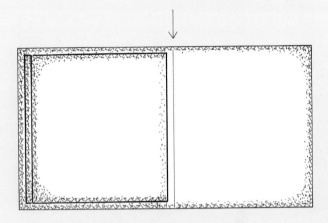

9   SEW THE FRONT SIGNATURE

Flip both signatures to the right side. Use the above procedure to attach the remaining signature to the cover along the left chalk guideline. The book is now complete!

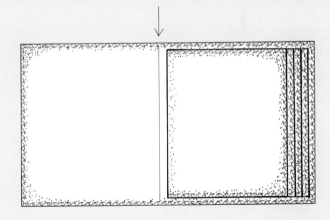

SIMPLE BINDINGS

Accordion-fold journals make fine display pieces, with extra support hidden inside to enable this structure to stand on its own. This journal shows off a collection of artists' trading cards with a childhood theme.

Support Fabrics

Buckram is a heavy-duty interfacing. It comes on a roll and is sold as a utility fabric in the fabric store. For concertinas that do not need to be self-supporting, lighter weight interfacing can be used for the interior support.

Concertina Journal

The concertina is an excellent journal for display because it is self-supporting, with a two-sided format that provides plenty of exposed surface for embellishment. This project features six panels on each side (twelve individual panels total) with a self-cover. Heavy support material added between the layers and a tightly bound finished edge make this structure suitable for a standing display.

MATERIALS

For a finished book measuring:
6"H × 24½" W × ¼" D
(15 × 61.3 × 0.6 cm)

- 2 PIECES BACKGROUND FABRIC, 6½" × 30" (16.5 × 76.2 cm)
- 2 PIECES LOW-LOFT, 100% COTTON BATTING, 6½" × 30" (16.5 × 76.2 cm)
- 1 PIECE BUCKRAM UTILITY FABRIC, 5" × 24" (12.7 × 61 cm)
- 100% COTTON SEWING THREAD

TOOLS

- ROTARY CUTTER
- QUILTER'S RULER
- CUTTING MAT
- SCISSORS
- CHALK MARKING PENCILS IN SEVERAL COLORS
- STRAIGHT PINS
- HAND SEWING NEEDLES
- SEWING MACHINE (OPTIONAL)
- STEAM IRON
- PRESSING SURFACE

1 PREPARE THE BACKGROUND LAYERS

Place one piece of batting on the work surface and add one piece of background fabric on top, right-side up. Mark the center vertical line with a chalk pencil on the background fabric.

2 DEFINE THE INDIVIDUAL PANELS

Measure 4" (10.2 cm) from each side of the chalk line and draw new vertical lines (A). Continue measuring 4" (10.2 cm) from each new vertical line until there are six 4" (10.2 cm) -wide panels marked on the background fabric. Join the batting to the background fabric by sewing along each chalk line with a straight stitch (B). Remove the chalk lines and press. Repeat steps 1 and 2 for the remaining fabric and batting piece.

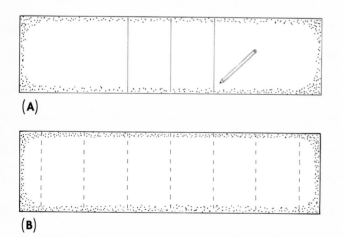

(A)

(B)

3 EMBELLISH THE PANELS

Complete the embellishment of all the panels. Press as needed. Keep buttons and other dimensional embellishments at least ³⁄₄" to 1" (1.9–2.5 cm) away from the long edges of the panels, and ¹⁄₄" (6 mm) from the stitched vertical lines, so that the panels will fold easily.

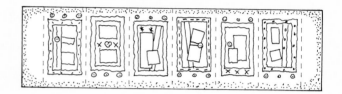

4 JOIN THE BACKGROUND LAYERS TOGETHER

Layer the two long embellished strips with the batting sides facing together. Check the orientation of the embellished panels so that the tops are in the correct position. Align the vertical sewing lines of each panel and pin them together along the stitching line near the bottom of the strips (A). Mark ¹⁄₂" (1.3 cm) seam allowance across the top long edge with a chalk pencil. Sew the two long strips together along the chalk line, using a straight stitch (B). Remove the pins and lift up the top layer along the seam line so that the batting is exposed on both layers.

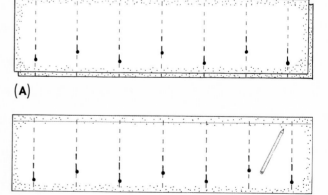

(A)

(B)

5 ADD THE SUPPORT MATERIALS

Add the piece of buckram utility fabric, laying the long edge close to the sewn seam of the top edge and the short edges within the outer pair of stitched vertical lines (A). Close the layers, match up the vertical stitching lines, and re-pin on each vertical stitching line as before. Sew through all the layers of fabric, batting, and buckram over the existing vertical stitching lines (B).

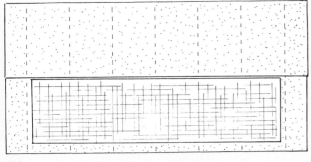

(A)

(B)

6 SEW, TRIM, AND FINISH THE OUTSIDE EDGES

Mark a new chalk line along the long bottom edge, 5½" (14.0 cm) away from the top edge of stitching (A). Sew through all the layers along the chalk line, using a straight stitch. Use the rotary cutter and the quilter's ruler to trim away the excess seam material, leaving ¼" (6 mm) on all four edges of the strip (B). Bind the edges securely using a zigzag, blanket stitch, or whip stitch along the edges. The blanket stitch provides a sturdy, neatly bound edge for a standing concertina fabric journal (C).

(A)

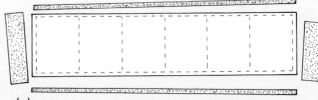

(B)

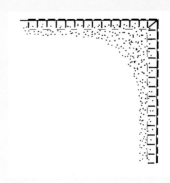

(C)

CONCERTINA TIP

• • • • •

All the panels on one side of a concertina are visible at the same time, so plan the color, design, and choice of embellishments accordingly.

SIMPLE BINDINGS

The buttons for this art journal were first sewn on securely to bind the book, then used as anchors for decorative fibers.

Button-Bound Book

This simple binding works well for thin fabric journals, adding a decorative yet functional element to the spine. Whole cloth pages are sewn to a separate spine piece to form page spreads, then spreads are joined to form signatures. Buttons are sewn through all the layers to attach the interior pages securely to the cover. Although the cover is slightly larger than the interior pages, both are constructed the same way. This journal has eight interior pages (two signatures of four pages each) plus the cover.

MATERIALS

For a finished book measuring: 6¾"H × 6" W × 1¾" D (16.9 × 15 × 4.4 CM)

FOR THE INTERIOR PAGES

- 8 PIECES CLOTH FOR THE PAGES, 6½" × 7¾" (16.5 × 19.7 CM)
- 4 PIECES CLOTH FOR THE SPINE PIECES, 2¾" × 7¾" (7.0 × 19.7 CM)
- 4 PIECES LIGHT TO MEDIUM WEIGHT NONWOVEN INTERFACING, 13¾" × 7¾" (34.9 × 19.7 CM)

FOR THE COVER

- 4 PIECES CLOTH FOR THE COVERS AND INSIDE COVERS, 7" × 7¾" (17.8 × 19.7 CM)
- 2 PIECES CLOTH FOR THE SPINE PIECES, 2¾" × 7¾" (7.0 × 19.7 CM)
- 1 PIECE LOW-LOFT 100% COTTON BATTING FOR THE COVER, 14¾" × 7¾" (37.4 × 19.7 CM)
- 1 PIECE LIGHT TO MEDIUM WEIGHT NONWOVEN INTERFACING FOR THE INSIDE COVER, 14¾" × 7¾" (37.4 × 19.7 CM)
- 100% COTTON SEWING THREAD
- 3–5 ASSORTED BUTTONS, ½" TO ¾" (1.3–1.9 CM) DIAMETER, FOR THE BINDING

Five unadorned buttons on the spine of this haiku journal reflect the theme of Asian simplicity.

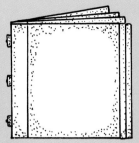

Telescoping, when interior page edges extend beyond the cover of the book, can occur when batting is used in place of interfacing.

CHOOSING SUPPORT MATERIALS

• • • • •

This project uses cotton batting to support the cover page spread, and medium-weight nonwoven interfacing for the inside cover page spread and all the interior pages. Interior pages that use batting will need to be slightly narrower than the dimensions listed to prevent telescoping. To substitute batting for all the interior pages, subtract ½" (1.3 cm) in width per page piece from the sizes specified in the Materials list. The spine piece dimensions do not change regardless of the type of support material used.

TOOLS

- ROTARY CUTTER
- QUILTER'S RULER
- CUTTING MAT
- SCISSORS
- CHALK MARKING PENCILS IN SEVERAL COLORS
- STRAIGHT PINS
- HAND SEWING NEEDLES
- BONE FOLDER OR CORNER TURNING TOOL
- SEWING MACHINE (OPTIONAL)
- STEAM IRON
- PRESSING SURFACE

1 JOIN THE SPINE TO THE PAGE

Pin one page piece to one spine piece, right sides together, on the long edge. Use a chalk pencil to mark ½" (1.3 cm) seam allowance along the long edge (A). Sew the two pieces together using a straight stitch. Press the seam open (B).

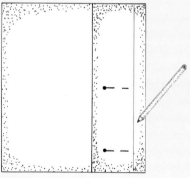

(A)

(B)

2 MAKE THE PAGE SPREADS

Pin another page piece to the remaining long edge of the spine piece, right sides together. Mark ½" (1.3 cm) seam allowance, then sew the pieces together using a straight stitch. Press the seam open. This forms a two-page spread.

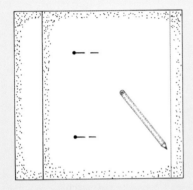

3 ADD THE INSIDE SUPPORT

Pin one piece of interfacing or batting to the back of the page spread. On the right sides of the fabric, stitch in the ditch along the spine seam for each page. Press. Trim any excess interfacing or batting from the edges of the page spread. Follow steps 1 through 3 to complete page spreads for all the interior pages and for the cover.

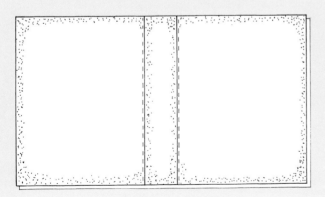

4 EMBELLISH THE JOURNAL

Embellish all the pages and the covers. Do not add dimensional or thick embellishments to the spine piece areas of the page spreads, because this area is needed for the binding. When planning the page designs of the journal, keep in mind that the pages will be nested inside each other when they are bound. The pages in a two-page spread may not appear next to each other unless it is the spread located in the centerfold of the book.

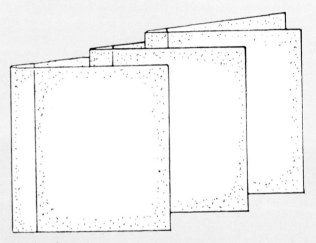

Nesting signatures

5 SEW THE SIGNATURES

Pin two page spreads together, right sides facing in,
matching the spine piece seams. Mark ½" (1.3 cm)
seam allowance with a chalk pencil on the top long
edge. Mark the two short side edges with ½" (1.3 cm)
seam allowances. Measure 6¾" (17.1 cm) from the top
chalk guideline to the bottom edge of the page
spread and mark a guideline approximately 3" (7.6 cm)
long from each corner. The unmarked area on the
bottom long edge creates an opening that will be
used to turn the pages inside out after they are sewn
together. Stitch on the chalk guidelines through
all the layers, using a straight stitch. This creates a
signature of four individual pages joined together.

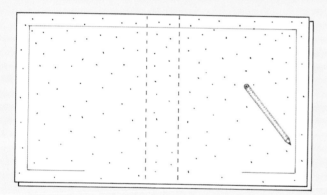

6 TRIM AND TURN THE SIGNATURES

Trim the seam allowance on the top long edge and
the two side edges to ¼" (6 mm). Trim the seam
allowance for the 3" (7.6 cm) area sewn on the two
corner edges of the bottom (A). Trim the corners
diagonally (B). Turn the piece right side out, using a
bone folder or point tool to square off the corners.
Press, turning the unsewn bottom seam edges to
the inside.

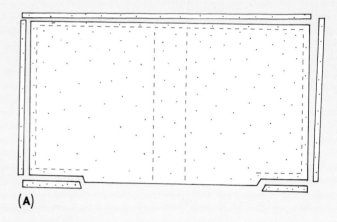

(A)

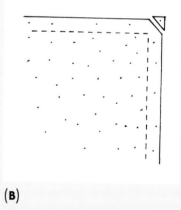

(B)

7 HAND FINISH THE OPEN EDGES

Use a needle and thread to hand slip stitch the bottom edge opening on all the signatures. Press.

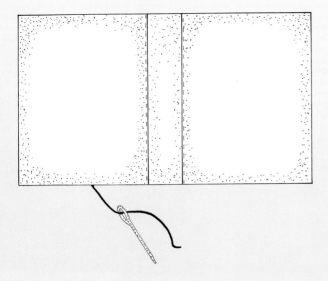

8 ASSEMBLE THE SIGNATURES

Create a stack of signatures with the cover facing down on the work surface and the interior signatures added in the desired order from bottom to top. Check the alignment of the spine piece seams for the correct position as each signature is added. Pin all the layers together.

9 AFFIX THE BUTTONS

Turn the pinned layers over so that the front cover is facing up. Determine the number of buttons needed for the binding and their positions on the spine, then mark the positions with a chalk pencil. Start at the top of the spine, position the first button in place, then sew it on securely through all the layers of cloth. Add the bottom button next, then the center buttons.

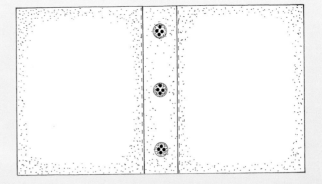

BUTTON TIPS

· · · · ·

- Use at least three buttons to secure the binding (top, center, and bottom); two for smaller size journals. Additional buttons can be added as a decorative element.

- Buttons can be sewn on functionally, with regular or button craft sewing thread, or with thick decorative embroidery floss such as no. 5 pearl cotton. Decorative fibers, including silk ribbon and many yarns, will not be strong enough to hold the buttons in place long term. Secure the buttons first with regular sewing thread and then add the decorative fibers as an embellishment.

Tape-Bound Journal

This lighter-weight journal is held together with twill tape. Signatures are sewn individually over shared tapes, which are pulled through buttonholes on the cover's spine, then sewn in place. The twelve interior pages (or three signatures) and lined cover are completely embellished before construction of the book begins.

Printed twill tapes can provide an instant title for a journal. Left uncut after sewing, the tapes can also become a closure by tying them together at the cover's edge.

MATERIALS

For a finished book measuring:
6"H × 5"W × 1"D
(15.2 × 12.7 × 2.5 CM)

- 6 PIECES BACKGROUND FABRIC, 10" × 6" (25.4 × 15.2 CM)
- 6 PIECES PELLON MEDIUM WEIGHT INTERFACING, 10" × 6" (25.4 × 15.2 CM)
- 1 PIECE COVER FABRIC, 12" × 6½" (30.5 × 16.5 CM)
- 1 PIECE COVER LINING FABRIC, 12" × 6½" (30.5 × 16.5 CM)
- 2 PIECES PELLON MEDIUM WEIGHT INTERFACING, 12" × 6½" (30.5 × 16.5 CM)
- 3 PIECES COTTON TWILL TAPE, 12" × ½" (30.5 × 1.3 CM)
- 100% COTTON THREAD

TOOLS

- CUTTING MAT
- ROTARY CUTTER
- QUILTER'S RULER
- SCISSORS
- CHALK MARKING PENCILS
- PINS
- HAND SEWING NEEDLES
- STEAM IRON
- PRESSING SURFACE
- TAPE-BOUND JOURNAL PAGE TEMPLATE, PAGE 135
- TAPE-BOUND JOURNAL COVER TEMPLATE, PAGE 135
- SEWING MACHINE (OPTIONAL)
- BUTTONHOLE FOOT FOR SEWING MACHINE (OPTIONAL)
- ZIPPER FOOT FOR SEWING MACHINE (OPTIONAL)

Making the Interior Pages

1 REINFORCE THE PAGES

Mark the vertical center of each background fabric piece with a chalk pencil. Place one page piece on top of one interfacing piece, pin together, and sew along the chalk line using a straight stitch. Repeat for all background page pieces, creating page spreads.

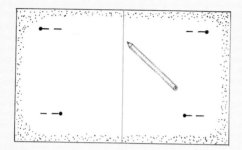

2 EMBELLISH ALL THE PAGE SPREADS

Complete the design and embellishment of all the interior pages before proceeding to the next step.

3 MAKE THE SIGNATURES

With the vertical stitch line as the center, use the quilter's ruler and a chalk pencil to mark a rectangle that is 9" × 5" (22.9 × 12.7 cm) on three of the page spreads. Place one marked spread on top of an unmarked spread, backs facing in. Pin the layers together and sew on the chalk lines through all the layers using a straight stitch, creating signatures.

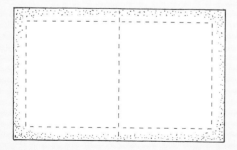

4 FINISH THE EDGES

Trim the outside seam allowance to ¼" (6 mm) outside the chalk line, using the rotary cutter and the ruler. Finish the edges with a zigzag stitch or other binding technique. Repeat for each signature.

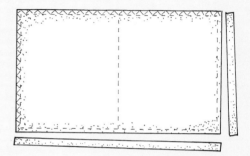

5 JOIN THE TAPES TO THE CENTER SIGNATURE

Select a signature for the middle of the book. Mark the tape positions on the signature's spine using the Tape-Bound Journal page template (page 135), or measure ¾" (1.9 cm) in from the top and the bottom edges of the signature and ³⁄₈" (1 cm) on each side of the vertical center point. Match the center of the length of twill tape with the markings and pin the tapes in place. Sew the tapes to the signature over the existing stitch line.

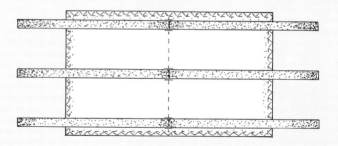

6 ADD THE FRONT SIGNATURE

Select a signature for the front of the book and place it on the work surface with the outside facing up. Fold the middle signature in half and align its center stitch line with the center stitch line on the front signature. Slide the middle signature to the left ¼" (6 mm), extending the tapes across the right end of the front signature. Pin the tapes to the front signature, and pin the middle signature layers to the left side of the front signature. Sew the tapes to the front signature along the existing stitch line.

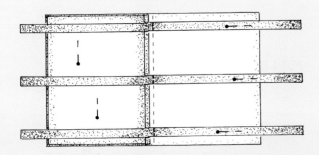

> ### TIP
> • • • • •
> Use the zipper foot for this step if you are using a sewing machine.

7 ADD THE LAST SIGNATURE

Take the remaining signature and place it on the work surface, outside face up. Fold the middle and back signature unit with the tapes on the outside and align it with the center stitch line on the back signature. Slide the unit to the right ¼" (6 mm), extending the tape across the left side of the last signature. Pin the tapes in place and sew them to the last signature along the existing stitch line (A). All the signatures are now sewn to the tapes, creating the book block (B).

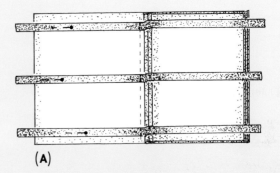

(A)

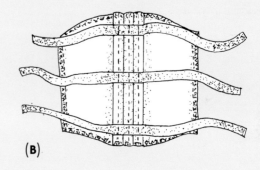

(B)

Making the Cover

8 DEFINE THE SPINE

On the right side of the cover lining fabric, find the vertical center and use a chalk pencil to mark guide lines ³⁄₈" (1 cm) away from the center on each side. Make a "sandwich" with the cover fabric facing down, two layers of interfacing, and the cover lining facing up. Straight stitch along the two chalk lines through all the layers, creating the spine.

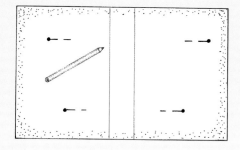

9 EMBELLISH THE COVER AND THE LINING

Complete the cover design and embellishment before proceeding to the next step. If you wish to embellish the lining as well, it will be easier to complete at this time.

10 JOIN THE COVER TO THE LINING

Using the stitch lines as a center reference, draw a rectangle 10¹⁄₂" × 5¹⁄₄" (26.7 × 13.4 cm) with a chalk pencil. Straight stitch along the chalk line through all the layers of fabric.

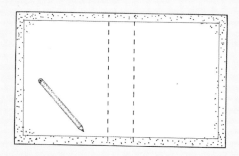

11 FINISH THE EDGES

Trim the seam allowance to ¹⁄₄" (6 mm) outside the chalk line and finish the raw edges with a zigzag stitch or other finishing technique.

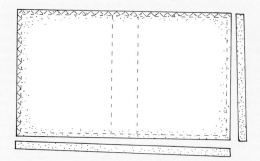

12 CREATE THE COVER OPENINGS FOR THE TAPES

Use the Tape-Bound Journal cover template (page 135) to mark the buttonhole positions on the cover lining (A). The buttonholes are ³⁄₄" (1.9 cm) long. Make the six buttonholes by hand or by machine (B).

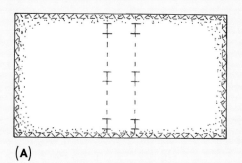

(A)

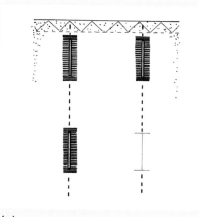

(B)

Binding the Book

13 ASSEMBLE THE BOOK PARTS

Place the book block inside the cover, centering the spines and aligning the tapes with the buttonhole openings. Insert the end of each tape into its corresponding buttonhole and pull it to the outside cover, extending the tape toward the cover's edge and pulling it taut. Pin the tapes in place.

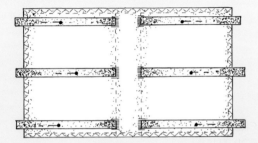

14 SEW THE TAPES TO THE COVER

Decide upon the length for the tape and mark the cutting point with a chalk pencil. (Allow at least 1½" [3.8 cm] for binding stability.) Open up the cover and straight stitch the twill tape to the cover along the tape's horizontal edge, across the cutting point mark, along the remaining horizontal edge, and finally along the edge of the buttonhole stitching, forming a rectangle. Trim the twill tape with scissors at the cutting point, close to the stitching. Repeat for the remaining tapes.

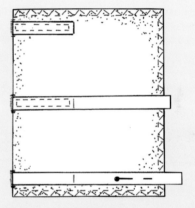

FINISHING OPTIONS

• • • • •

- Two or more of the twill tapes can be left uncut on the cover after sewing and used to fashion a closure.

- For a decorative spine binding, do not sew the tapes to the cover. Instead, tie the front cover tapes to their corresponding back cover tapes on the spine, using a square or decorative knot.

- Substitute grosgrain ribbon or other sturdy ribbon for the twill tape. Adjust the length of the buttonholes to fit the width of the ribbon, plus ¼" (6 mm) extra length.

- Additions to the embellished pages can be made after the journal is sewn by using fusible material or fabric adhesives.

INTERMEDIATE BINDINGS

This delicate bride's journal, made from simple muslin and cotton cord, acquires rich texture and depth on the spine from the French-Stitch binding.

French-Stitch Journal

The French-Stitch Journal is based on a traditional paper bookbinding technique. Rather than cover the sewing, the exposed spine in our fabric version shows off the intricate linking characteristics of the French stitch. The style is a good choice for journals with many signatures, because the binding can be continued beyond the five signatures (twenty pages) used for the example. It can be displayed in a standing position if batting is used as the support for the inside pages.

MATERIALS

For a finished book measuring:
5½"H × 5½"W × 1½"D
(13.8 × 13.8 × 3.8 CM)

- 10 PAGE PIECES OF BACK-GROUND FABRIC, 11" × 6" (27.9 × 15.2 CM)
- 10 PIECES BATTING OR INTERFACING, 11" × 6" (27.9 × 15.2 CM)
- 100% COTTON SEWING THREAD
- 1 YARD COTTON CABLE CORD, APPROXIMATELY ⅛" (3 MM) DIAMETER

TOOLS

- CUTTING MAT
- ROTARY CUTTER
- QUILTER'S RULER
- STRAIGHT PINS
- CHALK MARKING PENCILS IN A VARIETY OF COLORS
- STEAM IRON
- PRESSING SURFACE
- HOLLOW PUNCH
- SMALL HAMMER
- LARGE PLASTIC SEWING NEEDLE
- FRENCH STITCH JOURNAL TEMPLATE, PAGE 138

1 REINFORCE THE PAGES

Mark the vertical center of each page piece with a chalk pencil guideline (A). Mark ½" (1.3 cm) seam allowance guidelines from each outside edge on five of the ten page pieces (B). Place one page piece on top of one batting piece, align the edges, and pin together. Straight stitch along the center guideline. Repeat for the remaining nine page pieces.

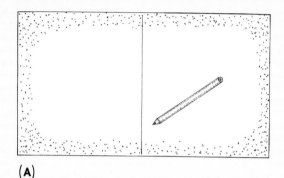

(A)

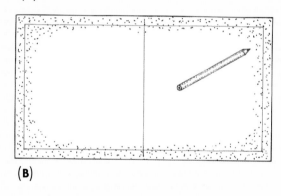

(B)

2 EMBELLISH ALL THE PAGE SPREADS

The right panel of one of the page spreads will also serve as the cover of the journal.

3 MAKE THE SIGNATURES

Make a page "sandwich." On the bottom, take a page piece with the center guideline marking only, and place it face down on the work surface. Place a page piece with the outside edge seam guidelines on top, with the markings facing up. Pin the layers together, aligning the center vertical stitching lines (a). Straight stitch on the edge seam guidelines of the first page "sandwich." Repeat for all remaining page spreads to create four more signatures (b).

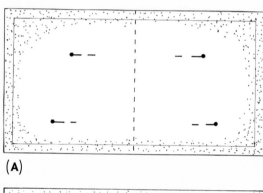

(A)

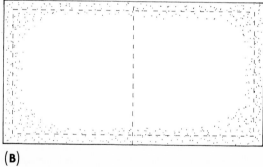

(B)

4 TRIM AND FINISH THE EDGES

Trim the seam allowance to ¼" (6 mm) outside the stitching line, using the rotary cutter and quilter's ruler. Finish the edges with a zigzag stitch or other binding technique. Repeat for each signature.

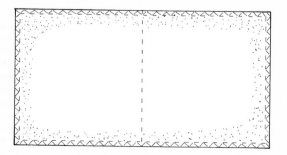

5 MAKE THE SEWING HOLES

Mark the positions for the sewing holes in each signature using the French Stitch Journal page template (page 138). Align the fold of the template with the center vertical stitching line. Use a hollow punch and hammer to create the holes. If eyelets will be used, set them after punching the holes.

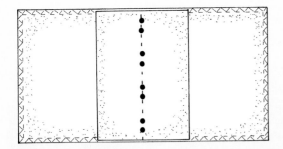

6 SEW THE BINDING

Arrange the signatures in order for sewing, with the front cover on top. Thread a large plastic needle with the entire length of cord. Begin at the top hole on the outside of the first signature. Leave a cord tail of 4" (10.2 cm) on the first hole. Use the running stitch and stop when the thread exits the bottom hole on the signature (A).

Place the second signature behind the first, lining up the sewing holes. Close the first signature and open the new signature to the middle. Enter the bottom hole of the new signature. Use the running stitch to exit the second from bottom hole, then loop the thread under the stitch on the first signature before entering the next (third) sewing hole on the second signature. Continue sewing and linking the stitches this way each time the needle exits the signature until you reach the top of the second signature (B).

At the top of the second signature, tie the beginning cord tail with the sewing cord in a square knot (C). Add the third signature behind the second and continue sewing, looping the cord through the previous signature's cord at each stitch along the way. Loop only through the cord of the previous signature, not through all intertwined cords. At the bottom of the third signature, link the sewing cord under the single cord that joins signatures one and two (D).

Add the fourth signature behind the third, and continue sewing and linking as before. Repeat until all the signatures have been added. Tie off the cord ends with a double knot.

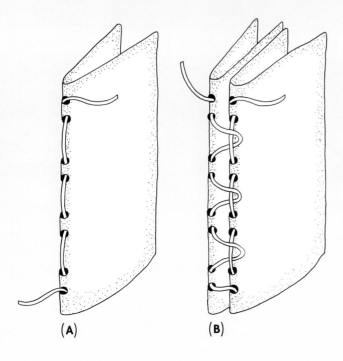
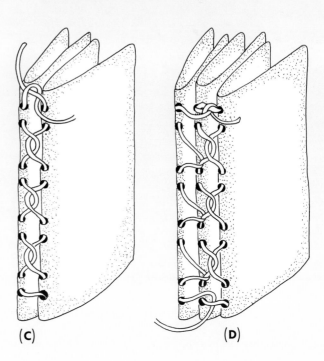

(A)　　　　(B)　　　　(C)　　　　(D)

This fun, dimensional structure shows all the journal pages at once, and is sturdy enough to support heavy embellishment on the exterior. The inside of the box provides more surfaces for design and the added bonus of a storage area.

House Box Journal

What if all the pages of a fabric journal were displayed on the outside instead of between two covers? Behold the house art journal, a box fabric structure with an interior compartment and six exterior "pages" bound together into a house shape. The roof is attached to the rear wall panel and folds back to reveal the interior. This project requires mostly hand sewing, although the wall, roof, and floor panels can be embellished with machine appliqué, embroidery, or quilting.

MATERIALS

For a finished book measuring approximately:
6¾"H × 5½"W × 5½"D (16.9 × 13.8 × 13.8 CM)

Note: Use the House Box Journal templates (pages 136–137) to cut the materials for this project.

- 100% COTTON SEWING THREAD

GABLE END WALLS

- 2 PIECES BACKGROUND FABRIC FOR THE EXTERIOR
- 2 PIECES FABRIC FOR THE LINING
- 2 PIECES LOW-LOFT, 100% COTTON BATTING

FRONT/BACK WALLS

- 2 PIECES BACKGROUND FABRIC FOR THE EXTERIOR
- 2 PIECES FABRIC FOR THE LINING
- 2 PIECES LOW-LOFT, 100% COTTON BATTING

ROOF

- 2 PIECES BACKGROUND FABRIC FOR THE EXTERIOR
- 2 PIECES FABRIC FOR THE LINING
- 2 PIECES LOW-LOFT, 100% COTTON BATTING

FLOOR

- 1 PIECE BACKGROUND FABRIC FOR THE EXTERIOR
- 1 PIECE FABRIC FOR THE LINING
- 1 PIECE LOW-LOFT, 100% COTTON BATTING

TOOLS

- HOUSE BOX JOURNAL TEMPLATES, PAGES 136–137
- ROTARY CUTTER
- QUILTER'S RULER
- CUTTING MAT
- SCISSORS
- STRAIGHT PINS
- HAND SEWING NEEDLES
- STEAM IRON
- PRESSING SURFACE

Making the House Components

1 BASTE THE BATTING TO THE EXTERIOR PIECES

Layer each exterior fabric piece on top of its corresponding batting piece. Baste around the edges on the seam allowance, about 1" (2.5 cm) away from the edge.

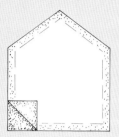

2 EMBELLISH THE PAGES

Complete the embellishment of the exterior pieces. Do not embellish outside the basting line, because this part of the fabric is needed to finish and bind the pieces together. Avoid heavy beads and buttons applied to the upper area of the gable end pieces, which need to stand upright in order to support the roof.

3 PREPARE THE LINING

Pin the corresponding lining piece to the back of each embellished exterior piece, with the right side facing out. Temporarily fold back the fabric layers on the edges with your fingers, and trim ½" (1.3 cm) around each outside edge from the batting layer only. Return the fabric to its original position, keeping the pins in place. Trim ¼" (6 mm) from each edge of the exterior fabric piece only. Do not trim the lining fabric piece. The extra fabric on the lining piece is needed for the next step.

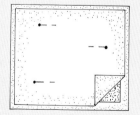

4 ROLL AND WHIP STITCH THE EDGES

Finish all edges completely before binding the pieces together to form the house structure. Roll the edges of the lining fabric of each piece (see page 53), turning under the fabric twice to conceal the raw edges of the batting and exterior fabric. Keep the rolls fairly tight. Roll until the fabric meets the 1" (2.5 cm) basting line. Whip stitch the fabric roll along the entire edge with the stitches about ¼" (6 mm) apart. Re-roll and adjust the edges as you stitch around each piece to maintain a consistent line along the basting stitches.

Joining the House Components

5 JOIN THE WALLS TO THE FLOOR

Determine the positions of the exterior walls on the house. Place the floor piece on the work surface, bound rolled edge facing up, and arrange the walls around the floor piece, rolled edges facing down (A).

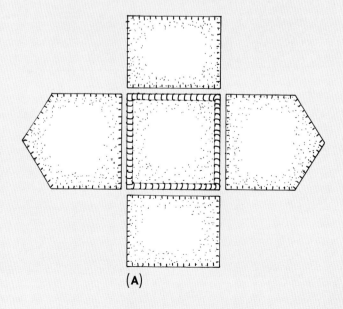

(A)

Turn over one exterior wall and lay it face up on top of the floor piece (also face up), matching the wall piece bottom edge with the floor piece edge. Pin in place. Whip stitch the two edges together over the existing bound edges. Take a few extra stitches at the beginning and ending points to secure the binding (B). Take the opposite wall and match its bottom edge to the opposite edge of the floor piece. Pin in place. Whip stitch the wall to the floor as directed above. Add the remaining two walls to the floor piece and whip stitch together.

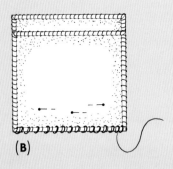

(B)

6 JOIN THE WALLS

Fold up two adjoining wall pieces, matching the bound edges. Whip stitch the two bound edges together, starting at the floor corner point. Repeat for the three remaining wall sides.

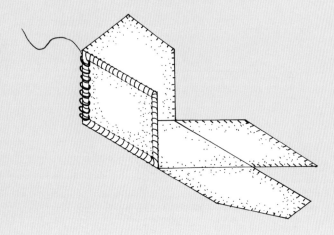

7 JOIN THE ROOF PIECES AT THE PEAK

Stack the roof pieces together with the linings face in, matching the edges. Whip stitch the two pieces together around the edge bindings on one long side, forming the roof peak.

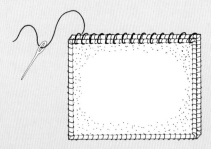

8 ATTACH THE ROOF

Place the roof piece over the walls, with the peak of the gable fitting within the fold created by joining the two roof pieces. The roof will overhang the house walls on all sides by about ½" (1.3 cm). Open the roof by folding back the roof panel facing you, while holding the back roof panel in place along the back wall edge. Pin the wall edge to the lining of the roof. Whip stitch the back wall to the roof lining, taking a few extra stitches at the beginning and end sewing points.

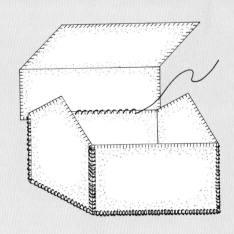

ADVANCED BINDINGS

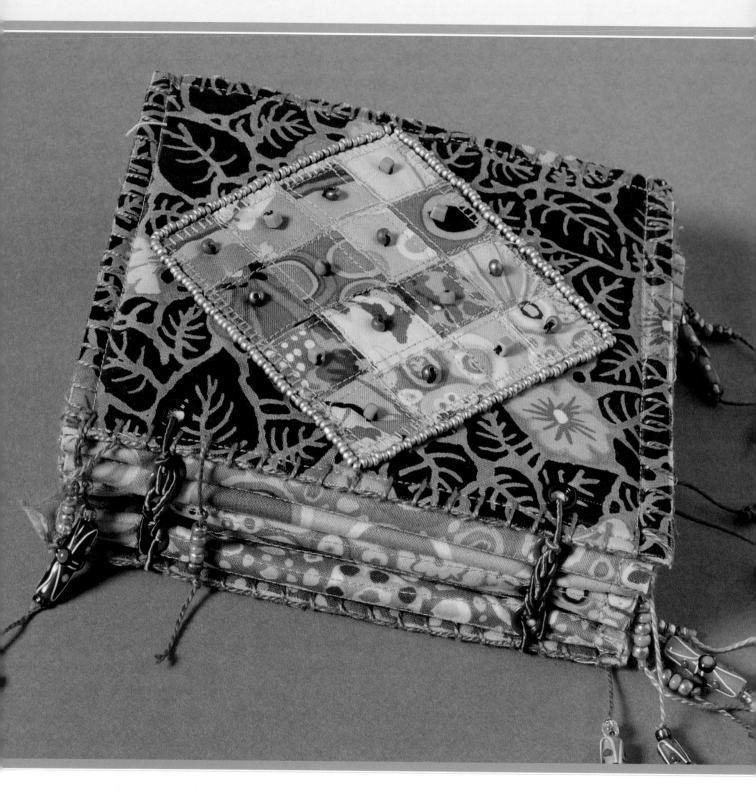

The Coptic stitch, a classic paper book binding technique, translates well for use in fabric journals. Tiny beads were tied on to the starting and ending threads of this journal's decorative blanket-stitched edges.

Coptic-Bound Journal

One of the earliest known sewn bindings, the Coptic stitch is a staple in the paper book artist's bindery. This version is sewn with two needles, one on each end of the sewing thread, in a paired set of punched holes. Sturdy covers enable the fabric version of the Coptic binding to stand up for display in the round. This journal has twenty pages and could be expanded to hold many more, but use at least five signatures to develop the decorative chain stitch pattern on the spine.

MATERIALS

For a finished book measuring approximately:
5½"H × 5½"W × 1½"D (13.8 × 13.8 × 3.8 CM)

FOR THE COVERS

- 2 PIECES COVER BACKGROUND FABRIC, 6½" × 6½" (16.5 × 16.5 CM)
- 2 PIECES COVER LINING FABRIC, 6½" × 6½" (16.5 × 16.5 CM)
- 2 PIECES TIMTEX INTERFACING, 6½" × 6½" (16.5 × 16.5 CM)

FOR THE INSIDE PAGES

- 10 PIECES BACKGROUND FABRIC, 6" × 11" (15.2 × 27.9 CM)
- 10 PIECES PELLON MEDIUM WEIGHT INTERFACING, 6" × 11" (15.2 × 27.9 CM)
- 60" (152.4 CM) ROUND CORD, ¹⁄₁₆" TO ⅛" (1.6–3 MM) DIAMETER
- 100% COTTON SEWING THREAD
- 4–14 FABRIC EYELETS (OPTIONAL)

TOOLS

- COPTIC-BOUND JOURNAL TEMPLATES, PAGE 139
- CUTTING MAT
- ROTARY CUTTER
- QUILTER'S RULER
- SCISSORS
- STRAIGHT PINS
- HAND SEWING NEEDLES
- CHALK MARKING PENCILS
- TWO CLOTHESPINS OR OTHER SPRING CLIPS
- HOLLOW PUNCH AND SMALL HAMMER
- TWO LARGE EYE HAND SEWING NEEDLES
- SETTING TOOLS FOR EYELETS (OPTIONAL)
- SEWING MACHINE (OPTIONAL)
- STEAM IRON
- PRESSING SURFACE

Making the Covers

1 EMBELLISH THE COVERS AND COVER LININGS

Complete the design and embellishment of the covers and the cover linings before proceeding to the next step.

2 DEFINE THE COVER EDGES

Mark ½" (1.3 cm) seam allowances with a chalk pencil on the four edges of the two cover lining pieces (A). Make a "sandwich" with the marked lining piece face down on the work surface, a layer of Timtex in the middle, and the cover piece on top with the design facing up. Clamp the sandwich together on two edges with the clothespins or clips. Turn it over so that the marked lining piece is now on top. Sew with a straight stitch on the chalk lines, moving the clips around as needed. Repeat for back cover piece (B).

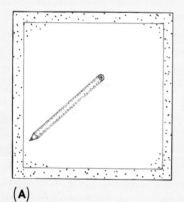

(A)

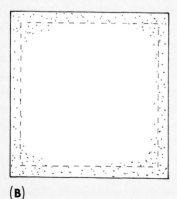

(B)

3 TRIM AND FINISH THE COVER EDGES

Trim the seam allowance to ¼" (6 mm) outside the stitching line. Finish the edges with the blanket, zigzag, or other decorative stitch.

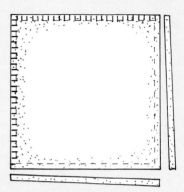

4 PUNCH THE SEWING HOLES

Use the Coptic-Bound Journal cover template (page 139) to mark the positions of the sewing holes on the spine edge of the covers. Make the holes with the hollow punch and hammer. If eyelets will be used, set them in the cover pieces.

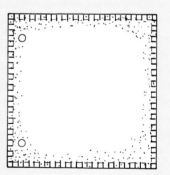

Making the Pages

5 CREATE THE SPINES AND PAGE SPREADS

Find the center vertical of a page piece. Mark a guideline $1/8$" (3 mm) away on the left of the vertical center with a chalk pencil, then mark a second guideline $1/8$" (3 mm) away on the right side of the center. Layer one page piece on top of one piece of interfacing and pin the two layers together. Straight stitch along the two chalk lines, joining the layers and defining the spine.

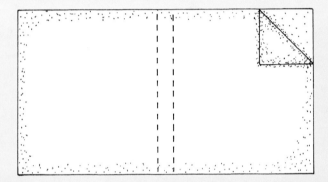

6 EMBELLISH THE PAGE SPREADS

Avoid adding dimensional elements on the defined spine area, because the sewing holes will be punched in this area later.

7 DEFINE THE PAGE EDGES

Measure and mark 5" (12.7 cm) away from the left stitching line on the page spread and 5" (12.7 cm) away from the right stitching line. Measure and mark guidelines for the height of the page, $5\frac{1}{2}$" (14.0 cm) tall. Position the guidelines so that the excess fabric at the top and bottom edge is roughly equal. Repeat on four of the nine remaining page spreads, for a total of five.

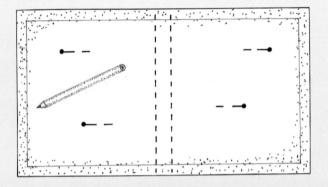

8 CREATE THE SIGNATURES

Make a "sandwich" with one unmarked page spread on the bottom, right side down, and one marked page spread on top, right side facing up. Pin the layers together. Straight stitch on the chalk lines, forming a signature. Create and sew four more signatures using the remaining page spreads.

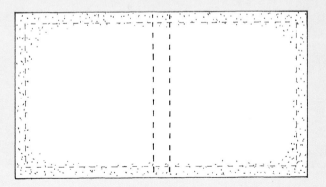

9 TRIM AND FINISH THE PAGE EDGES

Trim the seam allowance to ¼" (6 mm) outside the stitching line around the edges of each signature. Finish the edges with the blanket, zigzag, or other decorative stitch.

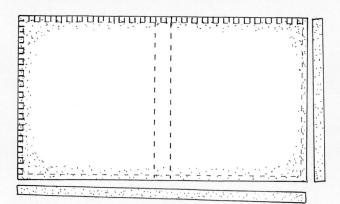

10 PUNCH THE SEWING HOLES IN THE PAGES

Use the Coptic-Bound Journal page template (page 139) to mark the positions of the sewing holes on the spine of each signature. Punch the holes with a hollow punch and hammer. If eyelets will be used, set them in the punched holes.

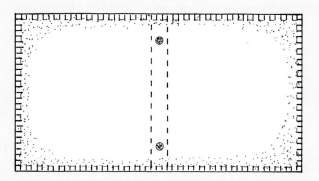

Binding the Book

11 PREPARE TO SEW

Stack the covers and signatures in the order in which they will appear in the final book, with the front cover on top of the stack. Thread each end of the sewing cord with a needle. Find the center of the sewing cord and pinch it to make a small crease.

Take signature one (which is the first one lying under the cover), open it up, and insert one needle into each sewing hole. Pull each needle with its threaded cord to the outside of the signature until the center point of the sewing cord lies midway between the two sewing holes inside the signature. The threaded needles now hang from the sewing holes on the outside of the signature with an equal amount of thread on each side.

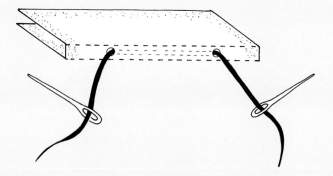

12 ADD THE FRONT COVER

Take the front cover from the stack and place it on top of signature one, in order. Hold the pair together with the front cover facing down.

Take one needle at a time and wrap the sewing cord down and around the edge of the cover piece. Enter the needle at the sewing hole on the front of the cover. Exit the needle on the back of the cover, with the thread falling between (inside) the two sewing holes. Wrap the cord around the first stitch by looping the needle out toward the closest edge and then behind the first stitch, locking the cover in place. Adjust the tension on the stitch so that the cord lays flat against the fabric. The threaded needles now hang between or inside the two sewing holes.

13 ADD THE NEXT SIGNATURE

Take signature two and place it behind signature one, in order. Enter each needle, one at a time, at the new signature sewing holes and pull the sewing cord through to the inside. Adjust the tension to create a nicely formed stitch on the spine, the first half of the chain. This step is sometimes called "the climb."

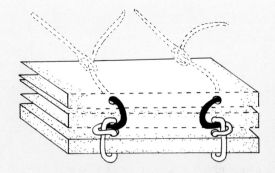

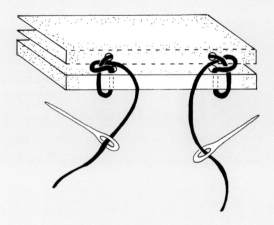

14 REINFORCE THE SEWING

Cross each needle to the opposite sewing hole inside the signature and exit to the outside. This time, the needles will fall outside of the sewing holes. This step is sometimes called "the crossover."

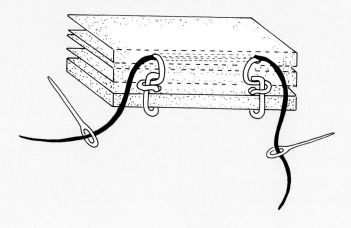

15 COMPLETE THE CHAIN LINK

Each needle now completes one chain stitch by linking under the previous sewing. Drop down two signatures (including the current signature that the needles have just exited) and pass the needle behind the stitches that attached the cover, moving from outside the sewing holes toward the center. Adjust the cord tension; do not pull it too tight. The needles now fall on the inside area between the sewing holes. This step is sometimes called "the link."

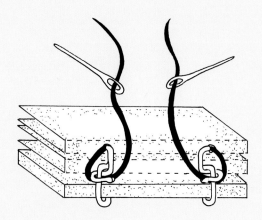

16 CONTINUE TO ADD SIGNATURES

Repeat steps 13, 14, and 15 (the climb, the crossover, and the link) until all five signatures have been added and the crossover stitch is completed on signature five.

17 ADD THE BACK COVER

Place the back cover behind signature five. Take the needles and wrap the sewing cord around the edge of the cover, then enter the sewing hole on the outside of the book. Exit the needles on the inside of the back cover, with the sewing cord falling outside the sewing holes. Wrap the cord around the cover stitch from the outside toward the inside, then pass the needle behind the cover stitch, locking the back cover in place. The needles again fall outside the sewing holes.

18 COMPLETE THE LAST CHAIN AND TIE OFF

Make the final chain stitch with each needle, dropping down two signatures (excluding the cover) and linking from the outside toward the inside. Reenter signature five with each needle and tie the two cord ends together with a square knot.

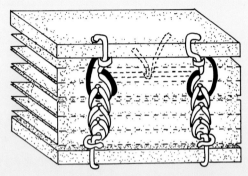

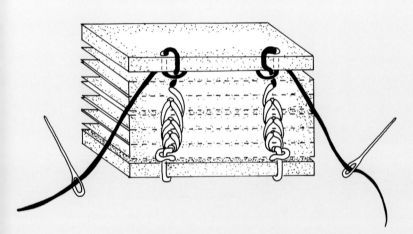

ADVANCED BINDINGS

This dream journal can function as a small decorative pillow on the bed during the day. Between the covers are plenty of paper pages to record dreams and those great ideas that strike in the middle of the night.

Dream Journal

This journal is a happy marriage of fabric and paper, with a soft, pillowlike removable cover and a substantial block of paper pages inside. The cover has corded piping around the outside edges, and two lined pockets on the interior hold the pages in place. The text block is French-stitched with decorative headbands on the top and bottom edges.

MATERIALS

For a finished book measuring approximately:
6½"H × 6¼"W × 1¾"D
(16.2 × 15.6 × 4.4 CM)

FOR THE FABRIC COVER

- 1 FRONT COVER FABRIC PIECE, 15" × 8" (38.1 × 20.3 CM)

- 1 INTERIOR LINING FABRIC PIECE, 15" × 8" (38.1 × 20.3 CM)

- 2 LAYERS LOW-LOFT, 100% COTTON BATTING, 15" × 8" (38.1 × 20.3 CM)

- 2 POCKET FABRIC PIECES, 6½" × 8" (16.5 × 20.3 CM)

- 2 PIECES LOW-LOFT, 100% COTTON BATTING, 6½" × 8" (16.5 × 20.3 CM)

- 2 PIECES BIAS BINDING TAPE, 8" L × 2" W (20.3 × 5.1 CM)

- 1 PIECE CORDED BIAS TAPE, 52" L × 2" W (132.0 × 5.1 CM)

- 100% COTTON SEWING THREAD

FOR THE INTERIOR PAGES

- DREAM JOURNAL TEXT PAGES TEMPLATE, PAGE 134

- 48 SHEETS COVER WEIGHT PAPER, 11" × 5½" (27.9 × 14.0 CM)

- 2-PLY WAXED LINEN THREAD, 4 YARDS (3.7 M)

- 1 PIECE CRINOLINE INTERFACING, 6" × 4" (15.2 × 10.2 CM)

- 1 PIECE BOOKBINDERS' DECORATIVE HEADBAND, 3½" LONG (8.9 CM)

- POLYVINYL ACETATE ADHESIVE (PVA)

TOOLS

- ROTARY CUTTER
- QUILTER'S RULER
- CUTTING MAT
- SCISSORS
- CHALK MARKING PENCILS IN SEVERAL COLORS
- STRAIGHT PINS
- HAND SEWING NEEDLES
- SEWING MACHINE (OPTIONAL)
- STEAM IRON
- PRESSING SURFACE
- BONE FOLDER
- 2 LARGE BULLDOG CLIPS
- HOLE-PUNCHING TOOL WITH A NEEDLE-SIZE POINT
- ½" (1.3 CM) GLUE BRUSH (FLAT, BRISTLE BRUSH)

Making the Covers

1 PREPARE THE POCKET EDGES

Place one piece of the pocket fabric on top of the pocket-size batting piece, right side facing up. Unfold the bias tape strip, align one edge with one long edge of the pocket piece, and pin it in place, right sides together. With a chalk pencil, mark ½" (1.3 cm) seam allowance along the edge (A). Sew through all the layers with a straight stitch. Remove the pins and fold the bias tape around to the back of the pocket piece. Press the sewn seam, then press ½" (1.3 cm) under on the remaining raw edge of the bias tape. Hand stitch the folded edge of the bias tape to the back of the pocket piece (B). Press. Repeat for the remaining pocket piece. Embellish the pocket pieces, if desired, before going on to the next step.

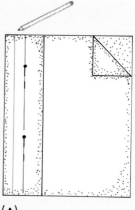

(A)

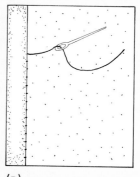

(B)

2 JOIN THE POCKETS TO THE LINING

Make a "sandwich" of one layer of batting on the bottom, the interior lining fabric piece facing right side up in the middle, and the two pocket pieces on top, with the bias finished edges facing the center. Allow 2" (5.1 cm) of space between the two pockets finished edges. This measurement is critical, because it is the minimum needed to insert the interior pages after the fabric cover is sewn. The pocket positions can be adjusted if needed to create the 2" (5.1 cm) space. Pin the pockets in place, then turn the "sandwich" over and trim any excess fabric from the two short ends so that the lining remains 15" (38.1 cm) wide. Turn the sandwich back to the right side. Mark ½" (1.3 cm) seam allowance around the outside edges with a chalk pencil and stitch the pockets to the lining.

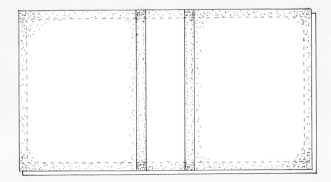

3 SEW THE CORDED BIAS TAPE TO THE FRONT COVER

Place one layer of batting behind the front cover fabric piece and pin it in place. Pin the corded bias tape to the front cover, matching the cut edges of the bias tape with the edges of the fabric and batting. At the corners, clip the tape in ¼" (6 mm) increments so that it shapes around the turn without bunching. Overlap the two tape ends by about 1" (2.5 cm), removing any excess.

To make the two cord ends fit neatly together, take one end and remove the stitching from 1" (2.5 cm) of the bias tape. Peel back the tape, and place the exposed inside cord alongside the covered cord on the other end of the tape. Clip the exposed cord so that it fits exactly with the other cord end. Turn under ½" (1.3 cm) of the raw edge of the peeled back tape and press. Layer the pressed edge over the other tape end so there is a smooth transition. Sew the corded bias tape in place, using ¾" (1.9 cm) seam allowance. Use the zipper foot attachment for this step if you are using a sewing machine. Press the cover seam allowance to the back of the cover. Tack down the seam edges at each corner with a few hand stitches.

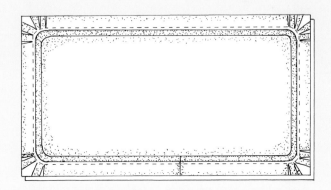

4 EMBELLISH THE COVER

Complete the design and embellishment of the cover before proceeding to the next step.

5 JOIN THE POCKET LINING TO THE COVER

On the pocket lining piece, trim the batting layer away from the seam allowance area to remove excess bulk. Press under ³⁄₄" (1.9 cm) seam allowance on each long end of the pocket lining piece. Pin the lining to the top and bottom edges of the batting side of the front cover. Hand stitch along the edges to join the lining to the cover (A). Fold under the seam allowance on one side edge and hand stitch it closed. Hand stitch the remaining edge closed (B). The fabric cover is now ready to hold the text block (C).

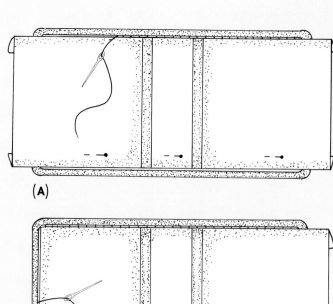

(A)

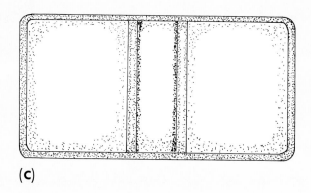

(B)

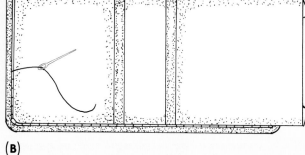

(C)

TOOL TIP

• • • • •

The bone folder, hole-punching tool, glue brush, and bulldog clips are useful tools for paper bookbinding projects.

Making the Interior Pages

6 PREPARE THE PAGES FOR SEWING

Fold each of the card stock sheets in half, one at a time, into 5½" (14.0 cm) squares. Use a bone folder to sharpen the crease. Assemble twelve nested signatures of four sheets each. Mark the front/top of each signature with a T in pencil; this will be erased after the book is sewn. Place the template inside each signature with the T of the template at the same end as the T marked in pencil on the front of the signature. Use the hole-punching tool to poke holes through the dots along the fold line, going through all four layers of paper. Punch one signature at a time until all twelve are completed.

HOW TO TIE A SQUARE KNOT

• • • • •

Right thread over left thread and under, then left thread over right thread and under. Tighten.

7 SEW THE TEXT PAGES

Sew the signatures together using the French stitch. Thread the needle with the entire length of waxed linen sewing thread and begin at the top hole on the outside of the first signature. Leave a thread tail of 3" (7.6 cm) on the first hole. Use the running stitch and stop when the thread exits the bottom hole on the signature (A). Place the second signature behind the first, lining up the punched holes. Clamp the two signatures together with the bulldog clips so that the middle of the new signature is open and the entire first signature is closed. Enter the bottom sewing hole of the new signature. Use the running stitch to exit the second to bottom hole of the signature, then link the thread under the stitch on the first signature before entering the next (third) sewing hole of the second signature. Continue sewing and linking this way each time the needle exits the signature until you reach the top of the second signature (B). At the top of the second signature, tie the beginning thread tail with the sewing thread in a square knot (C).

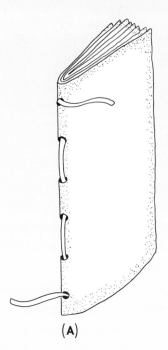

(A)

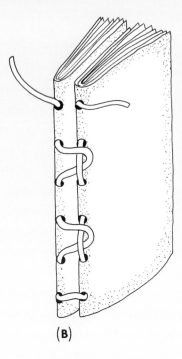

(B)

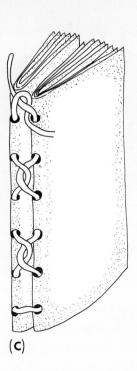

(C)

Unclamp the signatures, add the third signature behind the second, reclamp, and continue sewing, linking with the previous signature's thread each stitch along the way. Link under only the thread of the previous signature, not through all the threads. At the bottom of the third signature, link the sewing thread under the single thread that joins signatures one and two (D). Add the fourth signature behind the third, reclamp, and continue sewing and linking as before until all twelve signatures have been joined together. Tie off the ends by taking the needle under the last stitch and then through the resulting loop as the thread tightens. Repeat. Clip the thread ends to ½" (1.3 cm) long. The signatures have now become a text block.

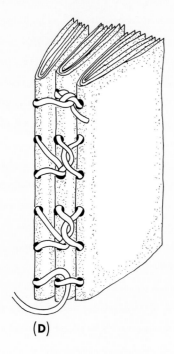

(D)

CRINOLINE

· · · · ·

Crinoline is a sturdy woven interfacing and is sold in fabric stores. It is not as stiff as buckram, but it has more body than most medium weight interfacings. Bookbinders use a similar material called "super" to reinforce bindings.

8 ADD THE SUPPORT TO THE TEXT BLOCK

Trim the piece of crinoline so that it is about ⅛" (3 mm) smaller than the height of the spine of the text block, and so it extends about 1" (2.5 cm) beyond each side of the spine. Stand the text block on its fore edge, and make it stable by adding a large bull dog clip on each side. Apply PVA with a glue brush to the entire spine area, then press the trimmed crinoline in place. Add more glue to the top surface of the crinoline, pushing it through the surface to the paper below. Allow the glue to dry thoroughly (A).

Cut the end band into two pieces the exact width of the spine. Glue one piece to the top and one to the bottom edges of the text block. The decorative ribbon of the end band should just overhang the spine edge (B). Apply glue to the crinoline wings on either side of the spine and press them against the adjoining page of the text block. Set the text block aside to dry (C).

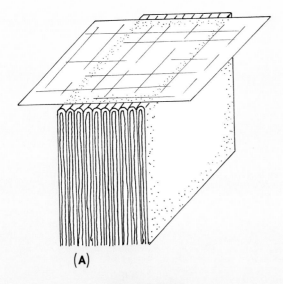

(A)

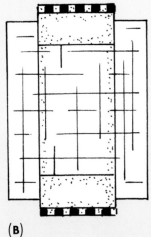

(B)

9 INSERT THE TEXT BLOCK INTO THE FABRIC COVER

Open the first and last pages of the text block and gently fold them back. Slide each page into a pocket on the fabric cover simultaneously until the paper edge reaches the back of the pocket. Carefully close the fabric cover, adjusting the position of the text block in the pockets as it closes.

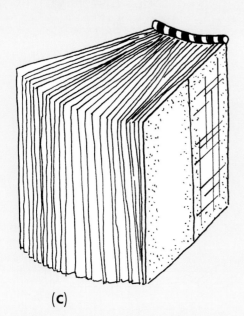

(C)

Chapter Four

GALLERY

"The only real voyage of discovery consists not in seeking new landscapes but in having new eyes."

—MARCEL PROUST

Your journey to make a fabric art journal wouldn't be complete without visiting others who have gone before you. In this section, you'll find a dazzling array of mostly fabric journals by artists who explore the art form following many different paths.

Some artists come from traditional paper book backgrounds; others are primarily art quilters who venture into fabric journals as another format for their art. Some are not book makers at all in the literal sense, yet their work communicates a story that could easily be told in book format. All of the artists have a definite sense of personal style and bring a unique combination of fabric art talents to their work.

If there is one theme that ties all the works together, it can be summed up as "attention to detail." What truly sets a fabric art journal apart from its paper counterpart, far more than the quality of the craftsmanship, is the choice and use of the materials. Savor the minutia of the examples found on these pages, and use them as a springboard to develop your own ideas for creating unique journals.

ARTIST: Jennifer Whitten

ARTIST **Keely Barham**

Fabric Persona Journals *(above)*
6¾"H X 4"W X 2"D (16.9 X 10 X 5.1 CM)

Three-dimensional figures that beg to be
touched adorn the front of these cloth-
cover journals. Arms and wings encircle
the back and become buttonhole closures,
wrapping around the paper page interiors.
Colorful velvets, fleece, flannels, and
cottons are richly embellished with simple
embroidery and beading techniques.
In addition to making beautiful fabric
journals, the artist is also an accomplished
doll maker who successfully incorporates
both passions into the project.

ARTIST **Keely Barham**

Willa *(right)*
6½"H X 6"W X 2"D (16.5 X 15.2 X 5.1 CM)

This tribute to an adored relative began
as a blank muslin journal. An extensive
collection of family photographs was
transferred onto cloth using an ink-jet
printer, then sewn on to layers of
vintage-style fabric prints using a variety
of hand and machine stitches. Buttons,
ribbons, and trims are lavishly used
throughout the book.

ARTISTS
Keely and Gerianne Barham
Hot Pink Journal *(above, left)*
6½"H X 6"W X 2"D (16.5 X 15.2 X 5.1 CM)

Hot pink and youthful exuberance
dominate this feminine journal, a mother/
daughter collaboration. Multiple image
transfers on each page are appliquéd to
the fabric background, then embellished
with heavy metal letters and large grom-
met book piercings. Arms on the stuffed
cover doll fold around the journal to
form a closure, joined by a Velcro dot.

ARTIST ### Keely Barham
Black and White Journal *(left)*
6½"H X 6"W X 2"D (16.5 X 15.2 X 5.1 CM)

Black and white is anything but boring
in this bold graphic journal. The artist
uses rubber stamps to create both text
and images, then adds dimension with
found objects, buttons, beads, letter tiles,
and photo transfers.

ARTIST **Keely Barham**

Soar Journal *(above, right)*
6½"H X 6"W X 1¾"D (16.5 X 15.2 X 4.4 CM)

Black serves as a dramatic background for gold, silver, and other metallic fabrics and threads used throughout this journal. Image transfers and other fabric scraps form whimsical figures, with small pieces of trim added to cover the points of transition.

ARTIST **Keely Barham**

My Voice Journal *(below)*
6"H X 7"W X 1¾"D (15.2 X 17.8 X 4.4 CM)

Small stuffed doll-like figures share an elongated cover on this journal with paper pages. Image transfers form the heads atop fleece bodies, which add tactile interest to the front cover.

ARTIST **Sally Adler**

ScrapBook *(left)*
Collection of Stephania Harden-Martin
8½"H X 5½"W X 1¼"D (21.6 X 14.0 X 3.1 cm)

An explosion of color and texture encases this fabric-covered journal with paper pages. Small bits and pieces of the fabric are collaged directly to the book board underpinnings with glue, while small beads, metallic wire, and threads are anchored to the top surface.

ARTIST **Sally Adler**

Chocolate Box with Shibori Pages *(left, middle)*
8½"H X 8½"W X 1¼"D (21.6 X 21.6 X 3.1 cm)

Tea-dyed muslin pages in this blank journal have a distinctive random pattern from the use of shibori techniques. The artist wraps unbleached muslin around a large diameter PVC pipe in a diagonal pattern, using cotton string to hold the muslin against the pipe. The fabric is then scrunched down to one end of the pipe and placed in a large pot of strong brewed tea for dying. When the desired color is achieved, the pipe is removed and the fabric is rinsed, dried, ironed, and rough torn into page-size pieces. Sizing or fabric stiffener adds finish to the pages.

ARTIST **Joy Osterland**

Shoes, Shoes, Shoes, Shoes *(below left, below)*
9½"H X 6½"W X 1½"D (24.1 X 16.5 X 3.8 cm)

The artist celebrates her favorite fashion accessory with a collection of thoughts on shoes. Beneath the hand painted fabric cover are the bare bones of a former textbook, its interior pages removed and the spine reinforced with duct tape. Fabric pages are sewn to new cover linings made of lush velvets and ultrasuedes, then embellished with rubber stamps and image and text transfers.

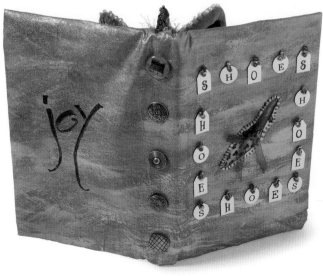

(A)

ARTIST Sas Colby

LifeBook 1976–77

12¼"H X 12¼"W X 1"D (31.1 X 31.1 X 2.5 cm)

Fabric journals may seem to be a relatively recent art form, yet mixed-media artist Sas Colby made LifeBook in the mid 1970s.

Hand-embroidered letters and linear machine stitching create the text and grid design. Vibrant scraps of silk form a rainbow of color (A).

Loosely woven cheesecloth is the background fabric for this hand-stitched family portrait sketch (B).

Photo booth pictures were transferred to cloth using acetone, then overembroidered to define features and clothing details (C).

Another acetone-induced image transfer serves as the base for further embellishment with a combination of machine stitching and hand embroidery (D).

The artist engaged her sewing machine as a drawing tool to capture this sketch of a devoted couple on satin, then appliquéd the piece to a background of well-worn lace (E).

(B)

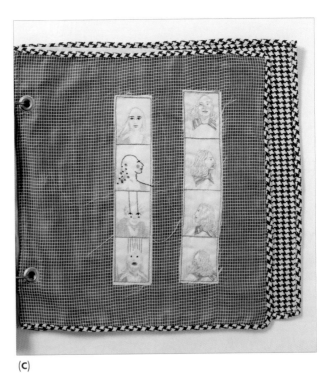

(C)

(D)

(E)

ARTIST Sas Colby

Hearts, Collection of R. A. Fanning
5½"H X 4½"W X 1"D
(14.0 X 11.4 X 2.5 cm)

This all-silk journal is a color feast for
the eyes. Very few words are needed
to interpret the ideas expressed—all
related to matters of the heart. Appliqué, embroidery, and the attachment
of small objects and beads give this
volume a precious feel in the hand.

The artist uses the transparent
qualities of the fabric to create a
pattern. On the left, thin organza is
sewn into a grid with uncut thread
tails adding color interest (A).

The shirt appliqué is cheesecloth;
the embroidered heart on its sleeve
provides high contrast to the magenta
silk background. Sewn onto a single
layer of fabric, this image serves
double duty on the back of the page,
where it faces a button dagger to the
heart (B+C).

Layers of color and emotion peel away
as the pages turn in this sequential
group to reveal a foolish heart at the
bottom layer (D).

A working zipper pocket slides open
to reveal tiny stuffed silk hearts that
appear ready to float away. (The
small stuffed hearts hint that broken
hearts can be stitched back together
again.) (E).

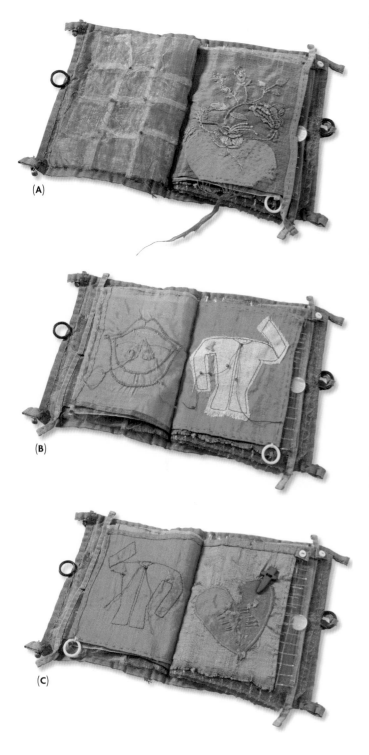

(A)

(B)

(C)

(D)

(E)

(A)

ARTIST **Beryl Taylor**

The Silk Book

6"H X 6½"W X 3½"D (15.2 X 16.5 X 8.9 CM)

China silk is the backdrop for this lush collection
of fabric and paper assemblages, bound together
with eyelets and a decorative cord. The artist's soft
color palette lends a dreamlike, ethereal feel to this
journal. Attention to tiny details throughout gives
the viewer plenty to digest without a single word of
text. On the front cover, layered shells and buttons
align on a square of linen.

A slim pocket holds tiny printed and hand-numbered
tags with the title of each page (A).

A small padded silk heart is wrapped with gold
wire and set to rest atop a frame of rubber-stamped
paper tags (B).

A different edge treatment on each page lends
exciting visual contrast not only to the individual
pages but also to the collection of edges displayed
when the journal is closed (C).

A repetitive pattern of buttons, beadwork, and tiny
tags rest on a silk square that is machine stitched
with a grid pattern (D).

A background base of hand-dyed cotton supports
silk panels that are embellished with sequins,
buttons, and beads, then attached with eyelets (E).

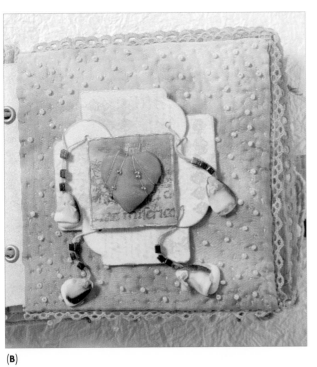

(B)

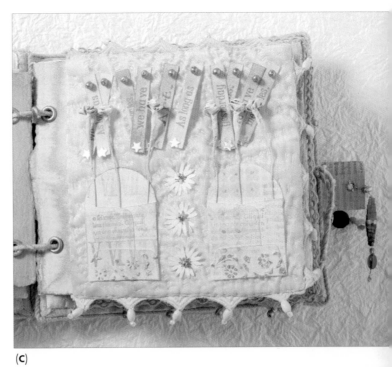

(C)

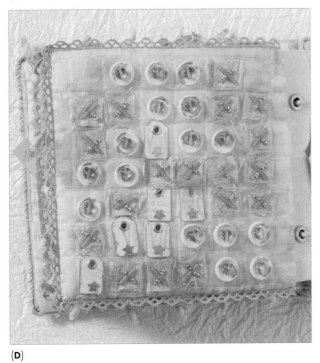

(D)

(E)

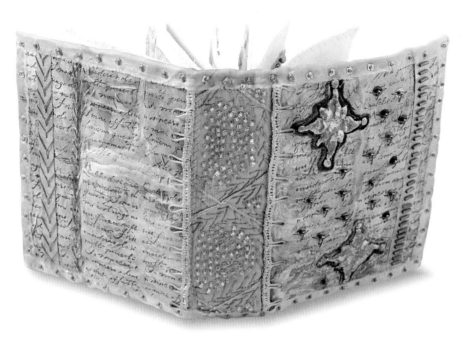

ARTIST **Beryl Taylor**
The Medieval Handbook
5"H X 4"W X 2"D (12.7 X 10.2 X 5.1 CM)

Soft and warm shades of lavender permeate the pages of this multimedia fabric journal. The cover is an unusual combination of Tyvek joined to a layer of tissue paper and hand stitched to a spine of silk.

Image and text transfers onto silk are the intermediate layer for this page spread. Torn strips of watercolor paper attached with eyelets hold the stem flowers in place (A).

The artist uses one central idea on each page and builds around a focal point. A figure is machine stitched to a piece of silk using metallic thread, then embellished with beads on each side. The layered paper heart is topped by wound gold wire, with tiny beads defining the page design border (B).

Latin letterforms are first stenciled onto the muslin pages, then outlined in gold thread with the sewing machine (C).

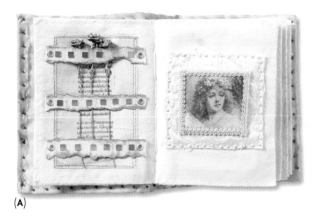

(A)

(B)

(C)

ARTIST **Geraldine Newfry**

The artist has taken a traditional binding format—sewing over tapes—and given it new life by using alternative materials in place of the standard cloth tapes. One journal uses a measuring tape as the binding medium, while the others are sewn over tapes made of paper-thin, liquid polymer clay that is rubber stamped and interwoven with ribbon. The high gloss surface of the clay is a dramatic contrast to the quilted cloth background and graduated color silk ribbons.

Measuring Tape Journal
4"H X 3"W X 1³⁄₄"D (10.2 X 7.6 X 4.5 CM)

Orange Quilted Journal
4"H X 3"W X 1³⁄₄"D (10.2 X 7.6 X 4.5 CM)

Green Quilted Journal
4"H X 3"W X 1"D (10.2 X 7.6 X 2.5 CM)

ARTIST Marian Crane
Continental Divide *(above, left)*
4½"H X 6¼"W X 2"D (11.4 X 15.8 X 5.1 CM)

Neatly embroidered text on tan linen alternates with appliqué work on patriotic print cottons to form the pages of this journal. The page edges are hand beaded and heavily fringed on the fore edge, in sharp contrast to the sleek wood covers. The appliqué images are hand painted and complement quotes and commentary throughout the journal. Inspired by the 2004 elections, the artist's book brings life to an original poem supplemented with quotes and commentary on religion, economics, and the environment.

ARTIST Marian Crane
Knots *(left)*
1½"H X 3"W X 1¼"D (3.8 X 7.6 X 3.1 CM)

This delightful miniature book is not much larger than the clothing labels used to form its interior pages, but attention to fine details and craftsmanship elevate its stature to something much grander. Leather and carved bone covers surround pages of linen and cotton that are hand painted, then meticulously beaded on the edges. The text is digitally printed and supplemented with tiny hemp knots affixed to the pages.

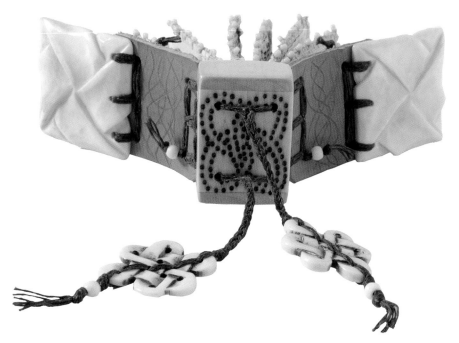

ARTIST Marian Crane

Color Play

7½"H X 6¾"W X 2½"D (19.1 X 17.1 X 6.4 CM)

A celebration of color and its symbolism is the subject of this journal with hinged fabric pages and wood covers. Long strips of linen at the top and bottom edges join the two parts of the hinged page, with the inner section featuring hand-embroidered text and the outer section displaying a concentration of Japanese glass beads.

ARTIST **Lesley Riley**

Paper Moon

8½"H X 8½"W X 1½"D (21.6 X 21.6 X 3.8 CM)

On the cover of this full fabric journal, a large-scale image transfer is the focal point, anchored by a log cabin quilt square. Inside, large letter stamps inked with white acrylic paint create text on a deep color background. A blue color palette dominates the pages throughout (A).

This journal was a traveling collaborative project, originated by the artist, with each participant contributing a page spread (B).

(A)

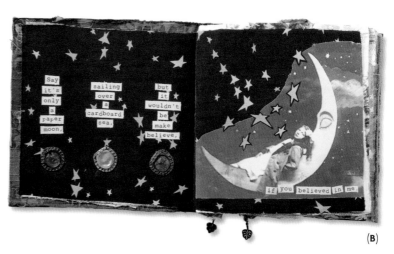

(B)

Trust
11³/₄"H X 15"W (29.8 X 38.1 CM)

ARTIST Connie Newbanks
Unbound pages

The fine hand of the calligrapher transforms a simple fabric page into a masterpiece. These unbound pages of text based on biblical proverbs are hand lettered with acrylic inks and thinned acrylic paints, using regular metal nib calligraphy pens. The lettering backdrop is hand painted and embellished with hand-carved images stamped with acrylic paint. The artist's selective use of small charms and buttons add some low-profile dimension and metallic contrast to the page design.

Marriage
15"H X 16"W (38.1 X 40.6 CM)

Children
16"H X 15"W (40.6 X 38.1 CM)

ARTIST **Jennifer Whitten**

Sun Dance Journal *(left)*
4½"H X 4½"W X 1½"D (11.4 X 11.4 X 3.8 CM)

Beading and embroidery work together in this small journal with cloth covers and paper pages. Basic embroidery stitches create the key design elements; seed beads, attached with the back stitch, fill in the front cover space. Covers are joined to the spine using the rolled edge technique, allowing the deep color of the lining fabric to add rich contrast to the bright cover.

Containment *(left, below)*
5¼"H X 5¼"W X 1¾"D (13.4 X 13.4 X 4.4 CM)

A collection of small found objects becomes a miniature gallery displayed throughout this fabric journal. Each page spread organizes the material into theme groups: keys, watch faces, paper cookie fortunes, postage stamps, and more. Displayed on a background of color-copied images from the artist's journals, each object is sealed in a clear vinyl pocket. Bias tape embellished with seed beads encases the edges of the page spreads.

Te Quiero Journal *(above, right)*
9"H X 6"W X 2½"D (22.9 X 15.2 X 6.4 cm)

A south of the border theme dominates the cover of this colorful journal with paper pages. Embroidery defines many of the design elements on the front, while a bezel of seed beads help affix the centerpiece, a Mexican pocket mirror with a folk art theme, to the cover. The design is adapted for the back cover, using French knots in a distinct color pattern in place of the mirror.

Pocket Journal *(below right)*
9"H X 8"W X 1"D (22.9 X 20.3 X 2.5 cm)

Fabric discoveries can simplify the bookmaking process by serving as instant covers. This journal began life as a reversible place mat, already finished on both sides. The artist created an inner pocket by folding the mat and stitching the outer edges together. A sterling silver chain and vintage German glass beads form a wraparound closure to secure the paper page contents.

Maternity Blessings
11½"H X 9"W (29.2 X 22.9 CM)

ARTIST Susan Shie

This colorful collection of small art quilts documents a time of change for the artist, from learning of her daughter's pregnancy through becoming a nanny for the new family, necessitating a temporary move to a new city. World events that transpired during this time also found their way into the work.

Starting with a fabric base of Kona cotton, the artist used an air pen loaded with fabric paint to create the basic drawings and diary entries. Once the paint was dry, the artist applied transparent textile colors with a brush to fill in the drawings, allowing the dark air pen lines to show through the color wash. The pieces are quilted and the edges are turned in and bound.

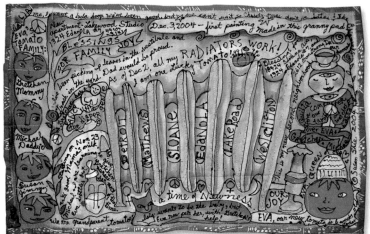

Radiator #1—Eva Radiates Love
11½"H X 18½"W (28.8 X 46.2 CM)

Three luscious ladies grace the cover of this multipage fabric journal that is actually a teaching tool. Each page of the book focuses on a particular embellishment technique, such as appliqué, beading, velvet, felt work, painting, and more. The pages were created individually and then bound into the book as they were completed. A fabric box holds the finished journal. The artist, well known for her delightful art dolls, has incorporated expressive faces and figures throughout the pages.

ARTIST Teesha Moore

le bebe *(left)*
12½"H X 8"W X 1"D (31.2 X 20.3 X 2.5 CM)

A velvet doll figure forms the base for this journal, with mixed media paper collaged pages that fold up when the button closure is opened.

ARTIST Teesha Moore

Two *(left bottom)*
12"H X 9"W X 2¼"D (30.5 X 22.9 X 5.6 CM)

Another patchwork journal has paper interior pages that are sewn directly to the spine, forming a random stitching pattern. A fabric collage with image transfer adorns the back cover.

ARTIST Teesha Moore

Wonder *(below)*
12"H X 9"W X 2½"D (30.5 X 22.9 X 6.2 CM)

This journal cover is an explosion of texture, the result of creating and assembling quilt blocks in an unexpected order. The artist took cotton fabric pieces and quilted, embellished, and bound the edges, then joined the blocks together with a whip stitch. A cascade of fibers on the spine was created by threading cut pieces of decorative fibers through a piece of hooked rug base cloth.

ARTIST **Teesha Moore**

untitled *(above, above right)*
9"H X 9½"W X 2"D (22.9 X 24.1 X 5.1 CM)

A beaklike appendage grows from the fabric
cover of this journal, complete with a shell mouth.
Inside, the paper-based pages are embellished
with fabric that is appliquéd using a sewing
machine and mixed media collage accents.

ARTIST **Teesha Moore**

Fabric Journal *(right)*
case 6½"H X 6"W X 2½"D (16.5 X 15.2 X 5.5 CM)
journal 5½"H X 5½"W X 2"D (14.0 X 14.0 X 5.1 CM)

A two-part journal and carrying case make a
happy couple. The case features a webbing handle
and button with loop closure on a fold-over flap.
The journal has a cloth cover and paper interior,
heavily embellished with image transfers, embroidery, appliqué, buttons, and fibers sewn directly
to the spine.

ARTIST **Pam Garrison**

Fabric Altered Book *(right)*
11"H X 14"W X 1½"D (27.9 X 35.6 X 3.8 CM)

This "shabby chic" fabric altered journal began
life as a 78 rpm record jacket. Vintage floral print
fabrics are loosely attached with brads to the hard
covers, and a variety of media, including fabrics,
create collage on the interior pages. A fabric
pocket on the front cover, fashioned from cloth,
holds paper doll images of the artist and her
project collaborator, Teesha Moore.

Templates

DREAM JOURNAL

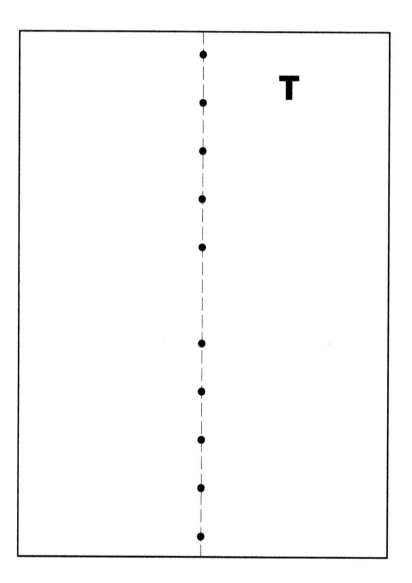

Dream Journal text pages
hole-punching template

page 102

Tape-Bound Journal
page template

page 80

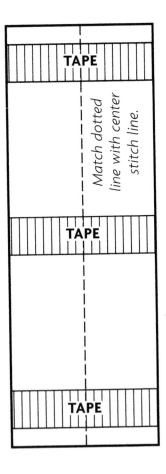

These templates are shown at 80% of the size needed for the project. Enlarge templates to 125% on the copier to get the correct size.

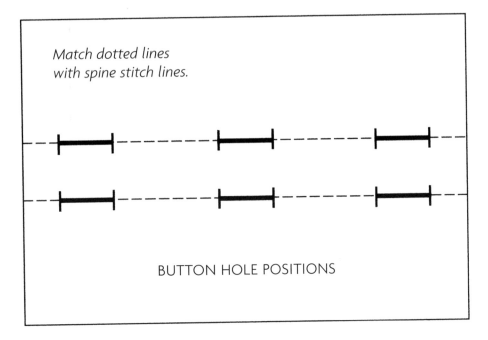

Tape-Bound Journal
cover template

page 80

HOUSE BOX JOURNAL

These templates are shown at 50% of the size needed for the project. Enlarge templates to 200% on the copier to get the correct size.

Gable End Walls template

page 90

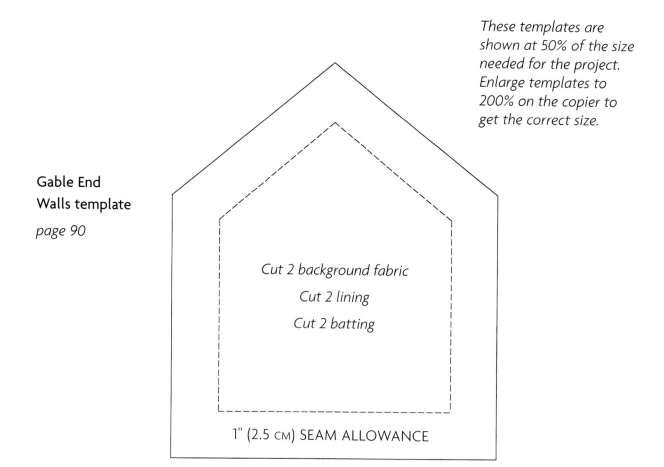

Cut 2 background fabric

Cut 2 lining

Cut 2 batting

1" (2.5 cm) SEAM ALLOWANCE

Front/Back Walls template

page 90

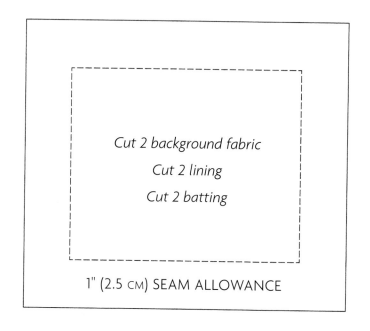

Cut 2 background fabric

Cut 2 lining

Cut 2 batting

1" (2.5 cm) SEAM ALLOWANCE

Roof template

page 90

Cut 2 background fabric

Cut 2 lining

Cut 2 batting

1" (2.5 CM) SEAM ALLOWANCE

Floor template

page 90

Cut 1 background fabric

Cut 1 lining

Cut 1 batting

1" (2.5 CM) SEAM ALLOWANCE

FRENCH-STITCH JOURNAL

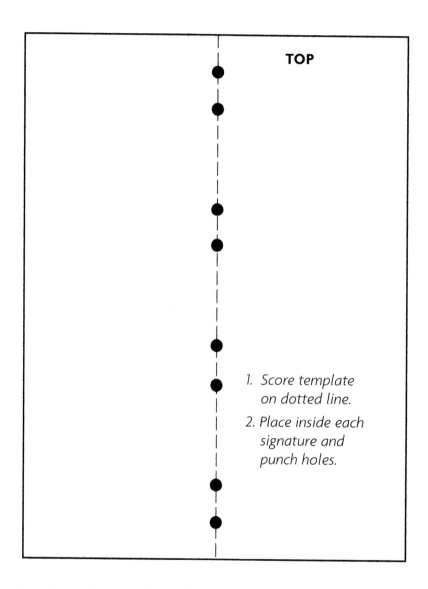

TOP

1. Score template on dotted line.

2. Place inside each signature and punch holes.

French-Stitch Journal template

page 86

**Coptic Binding
cover template**

page 94

1. *Align left edge of template
   with left edge of cover.*
2. *Punch holes.*

**Coptic Binding
page template**

page 94

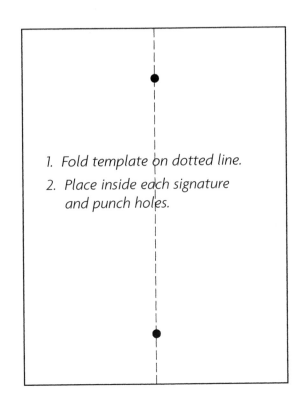

1. *Fold template on dotted line.*
2. *Place inside each signature
   and punch holes.*

*These templates are
shown at 66% of the size
needed for the project.
Enlarge templates to
150% on the copier to
get the correct size.*

RESOURCES

Acey Deucy
P. O. Box 194
Ancram, NY 12502 USA
rubber stamp images, Catalog $5

Anima Designs
www.animadesigns.com
rubber stamp images, ephemera

Blumenthal Craft
Blumenthal-Lansing Company
www.buttonsplus.com
buttons, photo fabrics, image disks

Bonnie's Best Art Tools
404.869.0081
www.coilconnection.com
*eyelet punches, eyelets, brads,
and other hardware*

Clover
www.clover-usa.com
*appliqué pins, bias tape makers, pressing
and marking tools, Asian knot templates*

Coffee Break Design
317.290.1542
www.coffeebreakdesign.com
*paper eyelets, brads, eyelet setters,
clear acrylic buttons*

Contemporary Cloth
866.415.3372
www.contemporarycloth.com
fabrics, books

Dharma Trading Company
800.542.5227
www.dharmatrading.com
textile craft supplies

The DMC Corporation
www.dmc-usa.com
embroidery threads and notions

Dover Publications
Fax: 516.742.6953
www.doverpublications.com
source for clip art and copyright-free images

Dymo
800.426.7827 ext. 2
www.dymo.com
LetraTag labelmaker and fabric tapes

Epson
800.463.7766
www.epson.com
*permanent ink-jet printers and
imaging products*

eQuilter
877.FABRIC.3
www.equilter.com
fabrics, books, notions

Fire Mountain Gems and Beads
800.423.2319
www.firemountaingems.com
beads, charms, and related supplies

Golden Paint
800.959.6543
www.goldenpaint.com
acrylic medium

The Hewlett-Packard Company
800.752.0900
www.hp.com
printers and imaging supplies

Home Depot
www.homedepot.com
painting tools and supplies, solvents

Houston Art, Inc.
800.272.3804
www.houstonart.com
OmniGel transfer medium

Jacquard
Rupert, Gibbon and Spider, Inc.
800.442.0455
www.jacquardproducts.com
fabric paints and dyes, alum, Calgon

Jo-Ann Fabric & Crafts
www.joann.com
tools, notions, fabric, and craft supplies

June Tailor
800.844.5400
www.junetailor.com
printer fabric sheets and iron-on transfer sheets

Junque
www.junque.net
rubber stamp images and alphabets

Lonni Rossi
610.896.0500
www.lonnirossi.com
typographic design fabrics

Lowe's
www.lowes.com
painting tools and supplies, solvents

Ma Vinci's Reliquary
www.crafts.dm.net/mall/reliquary
rubber stamp images and alphabets

Michaels,
The Arts & Crafts Store
www.michaels.com
arts and craft supplies

Patti's Stargazers
858.484.5118
www.pmcdesigns.com
patterns for A Stargaze Stitchery Tome

Postmodern Design
405.321.3176
email: postmoderndesign@aol.com
rubber stamp images, alphabets, and quotes

Stampers Anonymous
800.945.3980
www.stampersanonymous.com
rubber stamp images, alphabets, and quotes

Stampington & Company
949.380.7318
www.stampington.com
rubber stamps, books, magazines, crafting supplies

St. Theresa Textile Trove
800.236.2450
www.sttheresatextile.com
fabrics, beads, buttons

Talas
212.219.0770
www.talasonline.com
headband material, waxed linen thread, paper bookmaking supplies

Treasures of the Gypsy
505.847.0963
email: GypsyTreasures@cs.com
trimmings, exotic fabrics, appliqué trims, patterns

Turtle Press
www.turtlearts.com
rubber stamp alphabets

Zettiology
www.zettiology.com
rubber stamp images, alphabets, and quotes

CONTRIBUTING ARTISTS

Sally Adler
6323 Douglas Street
Pittsburgh, PA 15217 USA
techne@andrew.cmu.edu
Sally Adler's work ScrapBook appears courtesy of Stephania Harden-Martin, Monroeville, PA, USA

Keely Barham
Fabric Frog Designs
6680 Leafwood Drive
Anaheim, CA 92807 USA
FabFrogDesigns@aol.com
www.itsmysite.com/FabricFrogDesigns

Sas Colby
2817 Ellsworth Street
Berkeley, CA 94705 USA
sas@sascolby.com
www.sascolby.com
Sas Colby's work Hearts appears courtesy of R. A. Fanning, Menlo Park, CA, USA

Marian Crane
Crane Designs
2849 E. Redwood Lane
Phoenix, AZ 85048 USA
filigree@qwest.net
Marian Crane is represented by Bill & Vicky Stewart, Vamp & Tramp Booksellers, LLC
1951 Hoover Court, Suite 105
Birmingham, AL 35226
Phone (205) 824-2300
mail@vampandtramp.com
www.vampandtramp.com

Patti Medaris Culea
PMC Designs
9019 Stargaze Avenue
San Diego, CA 92129 USA
patti@pmcdesigns.com
www.pmcdesigns.com

Pam Garrison
31791 Via Patito
Coto de Caza, CA 92679 USA
pmdgarrison@cox.net

Teesha Moore
Alternative Arts Productions
Box 3329
Renton, WA 98056 USA
artgirl777@aol.com
www.teeshamoore.com

Connie Newbanks
Calligraphics, Etc.
916 Brookwood Drive
New Albany, IN 47150 USA
connienewbanks@insightbb.com

Geraldine Newfry
1437 West Carmen Avenue
Chicago, IL 60640 USA
geraldine@newfry.com
www.newfry.com

Joy Osterland
5740 Belleview
East China, MI 48054 USA
rosterland810@sbcglobal.net

Lesley Riley
7814 Hampden Lane
Bethesda, MD 20814 USA
LRileyart@aol.com
www.LaLasLand.com
Lesley is author of Quilted Memories: Journaling, Scrapbooking & Creating Keepsakes with Fabric *(Sterling/Chapelle, 2005)*

Susan Shie
2612 Armstrong Drive
Wooster, OH 44691 USA
susanshie@cox.net
www.turtlemoon.com

Pam Sussman
228 Ash Court
Wexford, PA 15090 USA
PamSussman@aol.com
www.pamsussman.com

Beryl Taylor
16 Merion Court
Monroe Township, NJ 08831 USA
berylptaylor@aol.com

Jennifer Whitten
13825 Courtland Avenue
Cleveland, OH 44111 USA
www.jenniferwhitten.com

ABOUT THE AUTHOR

Pam Sussman, a book artist since 1995, devotes her full time to teaching, writing, and making artist's books in fabric and paper.

Pam majored in design at the Art Academy of Cincinnati and, after a sixteen-year career in public relations at Procter & Gamble, operated a freelance graphic design business in Cincinnati for many years. As her interests migrated toward making hand-crafted books, she began to study bookmaking with Shereen LaPlantz and to produce small edition artist's books. Her early work led to invitations to teach, and for many years she taught book arts classes with Gayle Burkins at the Creative Block in Westlake, Ohio, and at special events in Cincinnati. She has given workshops every year at Art Continuum, an annual week-long conference of classes and exhibits for artists held in Cleveland.

Pam later operated a book arts studio at the Pendleton Art Center in Cincinnati, where she taught classes to adults and produced limited edition books. She moved to Pittsburgh in 2001, and shortly after signed on as a book arts instructor at the Society for Contemporary Craft, where she continues to teach. Pam has served as artist-in-residence at Pittsburgh Classical Academy since 2002, and serves on the special studies faculty at Chautauqua Institution, New York. Her students come from across the U. S., Canada, and Australia.

Her interest in working with nontraditional materials for traditional bindings led to her exploration of fabrics to create unique art journals. Pam's work has been published in *Artists' Journals and Sketchbooks* (Rockport Publishers, 2004) and in magazines, including *Observation* and the former *Taballae Ansatae*.

Pam lives in Pittsburgh with her husband, Richard, who is also an author of books on innovation for business. They have two children, Lilly and Elliott.

ACKNOWLEDGMENTS

Many friends, old and new, and family made significant contributions to this book. I thank each of you for the role you played in making it a reality.

First, to my parents, for nurturing those early creative urges. When I was a child, my dad returned home from business trips with wonderful surprises in his big suitcase: sets of colored pencils and canvas paint-by-number kits. Early summers were spent learning how to embroider with my mom. When she inherited her mother's treadle sewing machine, I learned how to sew clothing and acquired a lifelong love of working with fabrics. Her mother's handmade quilts now hang in my library.

Next, I could not have hoped for a better editor than Mary Ann Hall. She guided me every step of the way, while giving me the freedom to make this first book all I hoped it would be.

My contributors were not only gracious but also delighted about lending their work for the Gallery. They brought the ideas in this book to life and have given our readers a continuing source of inspiration for their own work. Thank you, thank you.

To Lynne Perrella, friend and now mentor, who first led me to Mary Ann and stayed for the duration. Lynne poked her head in my cyber screen door every now and then to ask, "How's it goin'?" and was a sympathetic source of advice and encouragement along the way.

To Ginny Carter Smallenburg, who has spent a large part of her life nurturing artists and providing the forum for them to practice their art. We began as business associates and continue as dear friends. Ginny extended that important first invitation to teach, and for years she encouraged me to write a book on my craft. Here it is, my queen!

To my son, Elliott, and my daughter, Lilly, for providing a steady flow of ideas and subject material for this and future projects.

And finally, to my husband, Richard, who was preparing his own first book for publication while I wrote this one. Thank you for inspiring me every day.